The Mapping of Monmouthshire

• • •

A Descriptive Catalogue of pre-Victorian Maps of the County (now Gwent)
• From Saxton in 1577 • with Details of British Atlases published during that period •

Robert Miller, 1821

The Mapping of Monmouthshire

A Descriptive Catalogue of pre-Victorian Maps of the County (now Gwent) from Saxton in 1577 with Details of British Atlases published during that Period

D.P.M. Michael

Illustration from the 'Reuben Ramble' 1845 to Robert Miller 1821 (opposite)

REGIONAL PUBLICATIONS
(BRISTOL) LIMITED

First published in Great Britain in 1985 by Regional Publications (Bristol) Ltd,
3 & 5 St Paul's Road, Clifton, Bristol BS8 1LX
and
5 Springfield Road, Abergavenny, Gwent NP7 5TD

ISBN 0 906570 18 2

•

•

Printed in Great Britain
Published in Gwent

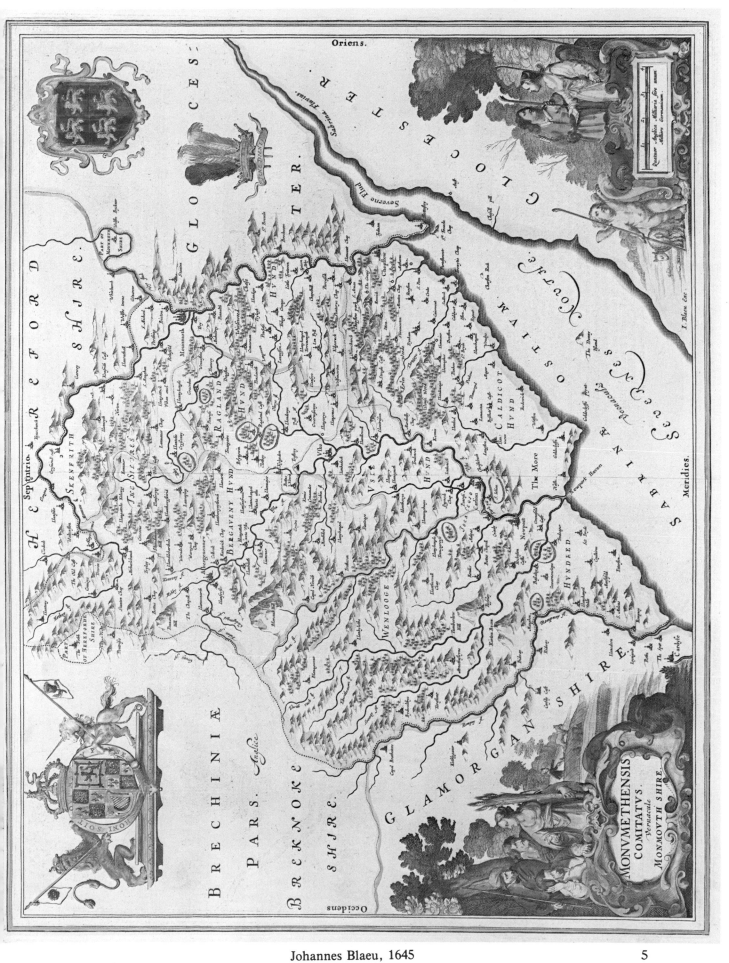

Epigraph

He had bought a large map representing the sea,
Without the least vestige of land;
And the crew were much pleased when they found it to be
A map they could all understand.

The Hunting of the Snark
Lewis Carroll

List of Illustrations

It will be noted that the dates are not necessarily of the first editions.

•

The cover design is adapted from John Speed's Map of 1610.

• • •

Contents

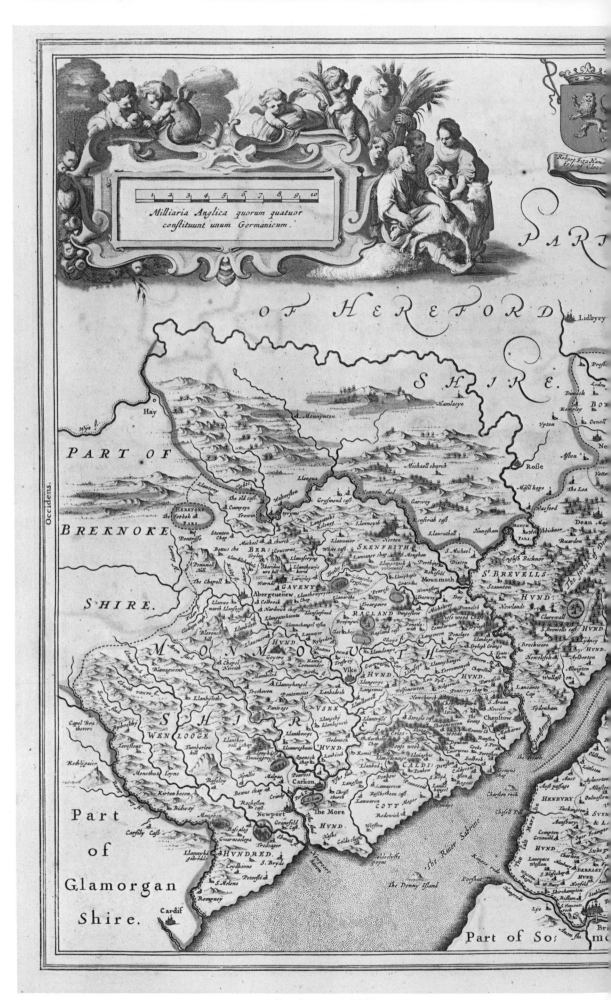

Jan Jansson, 1646

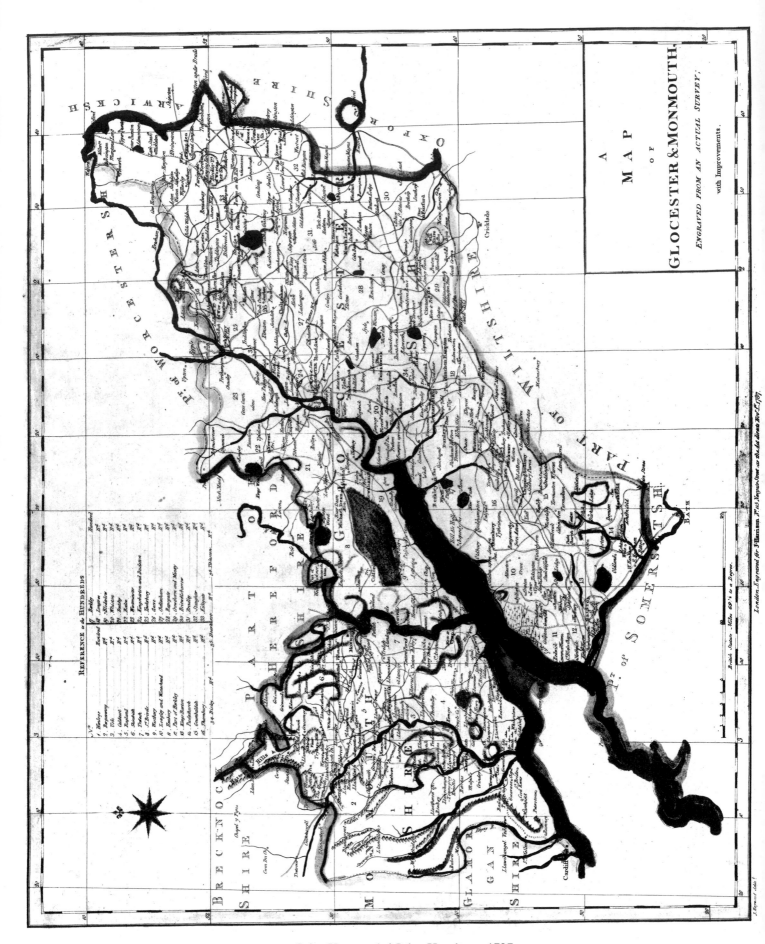

John Haywood / John Harrison, 1787

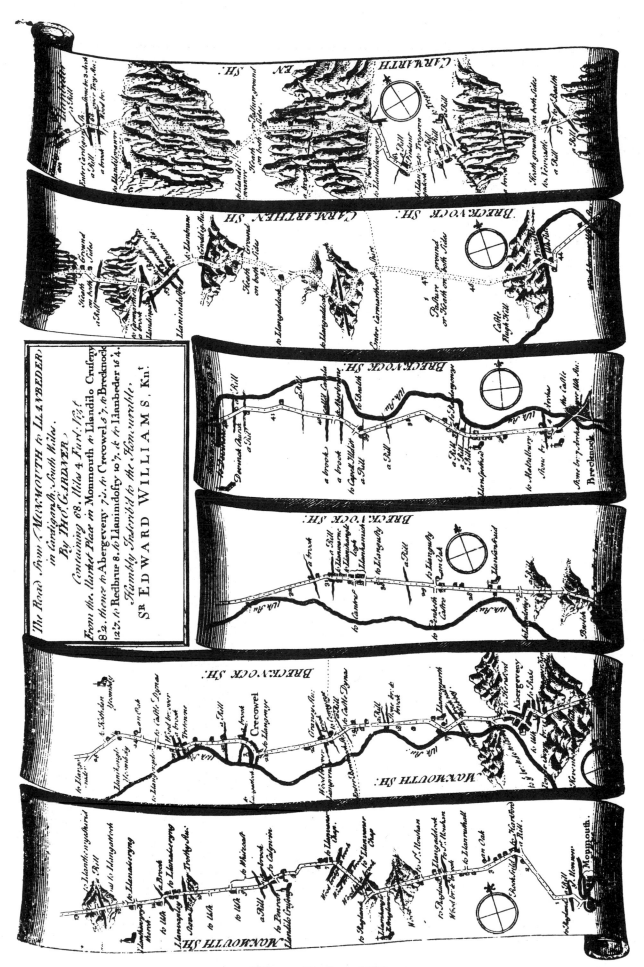

The Road from MONMOUTH to LLANBEDER
in Cardiganh, South Wales.
By Thos. GARDNER.
Containing 68. Miles 4 Furl. 1/2.
From the Market Place in Monmouth to Llandilo Crufeny
8 1/2. thence to Abergeveny 7 1/2. to Crecowel 6 3/4. to Brecknock
12 1/2. to Redbrur 8. to Llanindofry 10 1/2. to Llanbeder 6 4.
Humbly Inscrib'd to the Honourable
Sr EDWARD WILLIAMS, Kn.t

Thomas Gardner, 1719

11

MONMOUTH SHIRE

By H. Moll Geographer.

A. Bergavenni Hundred
B. Skenfrith H.
C. Ragland H.
D. wenloge H.
E. Uske H.
F. Caldicott H.

PART of HEREFORD SHIRE

P. of BRECNOCK SH.

P. of GLO~

CESTER SH.

PART OF GLAMORGAN SHIRE

MONMOUTH

Chepstow

Newport or Isca Haven

Cardiff

Severn River

3 Degrees West from London

English Miles
0 1 2 3 4 5 ... 10

Roman Fibula found at Kaer Lheion

This Represents another View of y same

The Fragment of an Altar found at Kaer Lheion

ISVSCI ILIVS.QI HATERIANVS LEG.AVG.PR.PR. PROVINCCILIC.

A Phiala or Bowl found at Kaer Lheion

A Chequerd Pavement found at Kaer Lheion

The Alabaster Statue found near Porth Shini

Map of the COUNTY OF MONMOUTH, Divided into Mineral &c. Agricultural Districts. By Charles Hassall. 1811.

REFERENCE TO THE HUNDREDS.

1 Skenfreth.
2 Wentloog.
3 Abergavenny.
4 Ragland.
5 Usk.
6 Caldicot.

REFERENCE TO THE COLOURS &c.

Mineral division — Indian Ink
Level division — Grafs Green
Hill division — Pale Pink
Mountain division — Dark Brown
Vale division — Pale Blue
The Red lines divide the County into Hundreds

BOUNDARIES

County
Hundreds
Soils

Scale of Statute Miles

BRISTOL CHANNEL

Samuel John Neele / Charles Hassall, 1811   13

This COUNTY contains 1 Borough and 6 Market Towns

Abergavenny. Market *Tuesd.* Fairs *May 14. first Tuesd. after Trinity Sunday, Sep. 25* . . . . . .

Carleon. Market *Thurs.* Fairs *May 1. July 20. Sep. 21* . . . .

Chepstow. Market *Sat.* Fairs

Whitsun Fr. Sat. before June 20. Aug. 1. Friday sennight after Oct. 18. . . . .

Monmouth *sends 1 Memb.* Market *Sat.* Fairs *Whit Tuesd. Sep. 4. Nov. 22* . . . .

Newport. Mark.ᵗ *Sat. Fᵗˢ Holy Th. Whit Th. Aug. 15. Nov. 6.*

Ponty-pool. Mar.ᵗ *S.* Fairs *April 22. July 5. Oct. 10.* . . . . .

Uſk. Market *Mon.* Fairs *Mon after Trinity Sunday, Oct. 18.*

Robert Sayer, 1787

14

Introduction

The purpose of this book is to supply a general background of information against which collectors and interested readers may profitably date and identify known specimens of maps of the County of Monmouthshire, now Gwent, up to and just beyond the introduction of the Ordnance Survey. This object is less limited than it would appear because Monmouthshire, alone amongst the Welsh Counties, was for some centuries in the anomalous position of being regarded as English and was therefore included in English County Atlases from the earliest date.

The maps of Monmouthshire described were therefore similar in style, date and dimensions, to corresponding English and, where they occur, to Welsh Counties. This means that the book contains not merely an exhaustive list of Maps of Monmouthshire from the 16th to the 19th centuries, but may also serve as a reference when identifying and checking a wide range of other County maps. An added bonus is that the book includes details of the principal pre-Victorian Atlases and topographical and historical works cartographically illustrated.

Anyone familiar with the work will at once recognise the author's indebtedness to Mr Donald Hodson's marvellously detailed guide to THE PRINTED MAPS OF HERTFORDSHIRE 1577-1900 (Dawsons of Pall Mall, 1974) and, inevitably, to Thomas Chubb's PRINTED MAPS IN THE ATLASES OF GREAT BRITAIN AND IRELAND 1579-1870 (reprinted by Dawson, 1977).

Descriptive lists of other Welsh County Maps 1578-1900, limited to copies in the National Library of Wales, have been published by M. Gwyneth Lewis: THE PRINTED MAPS OF BRECONSHIRE, OF RADNORSHIRE; OF CARDIGANSHIRE; OF MERIONETHSHIRE.

The disadvantage of the foregoing books is that they are short of or lacking in illustrative material. John Booth's readable ANTIQUE MAPS OF WALES (1977) is well illustrated, but makes no claim to be comprehensive in any respect.

My principal debt is to Mr Alan Hodgkiss, author of UNDERSTANDING MAPS: A SYSTEMATIC HISTORY OF THEIR USE AND DEVELOPMENT (Dawson, 1981) and DISCOVERING ANTIQUE MAPS (Shire Publications, 1971). He has read my manuscript and made many valuable suggestions, most of which I have gratefully adopted. Remaining errors and omissions are entirely mine.

Although almost all the maps of Monmouthshire (Gwent) discussed and illustrated are in my own collection, I have benefited hugely from the inspection of maps and other relevant materials in public depositories. At the National Library of Wales, Aberystwyth, my chief mentor has been Mr Robert Davies, Assistant Keeper in the Department of Prints, Drawings and Maps. Visits to the British Library in London and to the Bodleian Library at Oxford have always been rewarding.

There have been useful contacts with the Gwent County Archivists, Mr William Baker and his successor Mr Delwyn Tibbott, and with officers of Newport's Museum and Reference Library. Finally, map-sellers everywhere have proved themselves to be most knowledgeable about their wares and ready always both to teach and to learn.

It is very much hoped that THE MAPPING OF MONMOUTHSHIRE will have, as intended, a wider use and a larger interest than the title of the book suggests.

★ ★ ★

NOTE: The Maps are listed in chronological order of first appearance, but re-issues and later editions are usually conveniently grouped and must therefore occasion some chronological over-lapping. Some endeavour is made, in identifying a particular map, to go back beyond the publisher or printer, through the engraver and the draughtsman, as near as possible to the originator, the surveyor. Unfortunately, Anon too often played a part in the earliest stages of cartography.

Maps including a county other than Monmouthshire are described only where Monmouthshire itself is drawn in some detail.

The vertical height of the frame within which the map is drawn precedes the horizontal measurement. Slight variations in size should be allowed for.

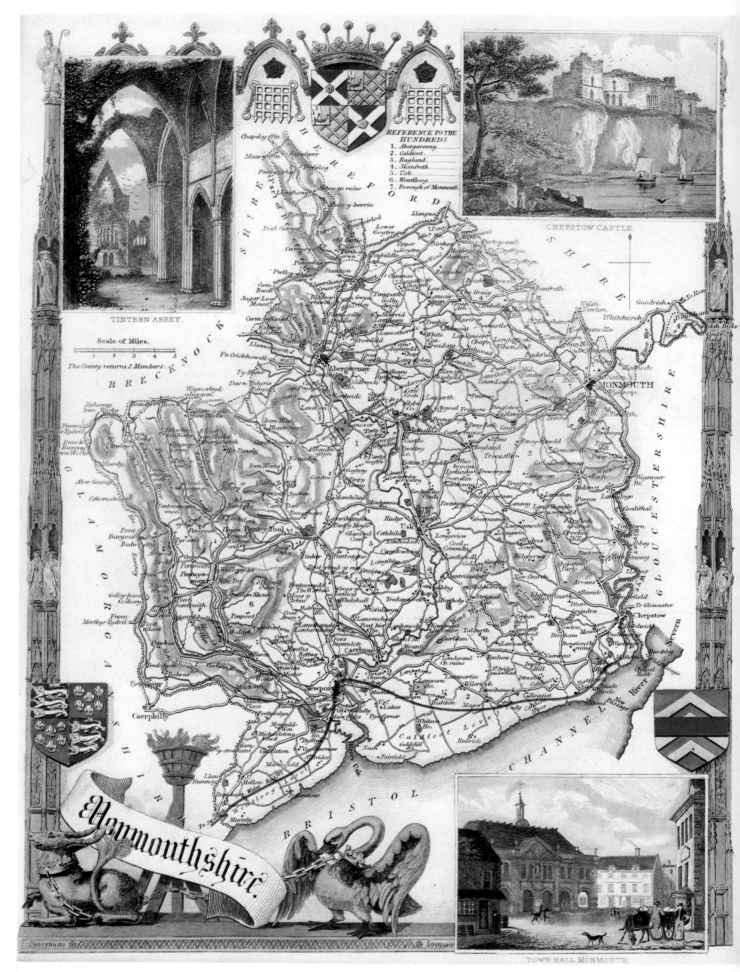

TINTERN ABBEY.

CHEPSTOW CASTLE.

REFERENCE TO THE
HUNDREDS
1. Abergavenny
2. Caldicot
3. Ragland
4. Skenfreth
5. Usk
6. Wentlloog
7. Borough of Monmouth

Scale of Miles.

The County returns 2 Members.

MONMOUTH

Monmouthshire

TOWN HALL MONMOUTH.

Thomas Moule, 1831

CHAPTER I

Map Making

Mapping began when the first primitive man or woman indicated in sand with foot or finger a crude direction or geographical feature. Maps began when it was discovered that clay, parchment, papyrus or paper successively could convey meaningful signs and symbols.

It remains a mystery how earth-bound people in remote times could visualise and sketch with any accuracy the outlines of land and water. In ancient Babylon, in Egypt, where the flooding Nile necessitated the recording of boundaries, and elsewhere in the Mediterranean regions, cartography painfully grew up in the long centuries before Christ into something more sophisticated than rough land surveys. Trade demanded simple sea-charts. Maps became a military requirement, mentioned by name by Herodotus in that astonishing fifth century B.C. when the Greeks founded almost all modern Science and Mathematics.

It is not easy to appreciate the vast problems that had to be solved before anything that could acceptably be called a map would be drawn. Stone-age men in the caves of Lascaux and Altamira drew creditable portraits of wild boars, horses and bison. They had the imagination to reduce the animal in size and keep roughly in proportion heads, bodies, legs. They even used shades of red and brown and black.

Mathematical exactitude in measurement and in scale took millenia to develop. Even in recorded history there have been somewhat elastic systems of measurement. The Roman mile, mille pasuum, comprises a thousand double paces and you may well ask, whose paces? It was 1611 English yards, or thereabouts. Before the statute mile of 1760 yards, the mile was variable. The earlier traveller would have been well advised to check whether he were being directed to pursue English, Scottish, Irish or Welsh miles. There were variations even within Counties.

The mile itself may be yielding to the kilometre, but many other exotic measures of length lie strewn along the international route: parasang and stadium, li and coss are relegated nowadays to crosswords and Scrabble. Less precise measurements like the sea-side landlady's *stone's-throw* are still in vogue. Giraldus Cambrensis long ago described the valley in which Llanthony Abbey stands as about an arrow-shot wide. The writer, walking many years ago in Devonshire, asked a countryman the distance to a particular village and was told that it would be about two gun-shots.

Without there being at least some approximation of measurement, a map is of little use. Scale is the ratio between measurement on the ground and measurement on the map. The greater the reduction in scale, the larger the area can be represented, but there is an optimum scale for any particular purpose. A country walker needs one inch to the mile to find footpaths; a motorist is normally satisfied with one tenth of an inch to the mile. It is generally convenient to represent the scale as a vulgar or decimal fraction. The metric system clearly facilitates decimal fractionalisation.

The measurement of an irregular area is simplified by triangulation. Simple geometry establishes the construction of suitable triangles to fill in the maximum possible area within the total irregular framework. The practice may even have preceded the theory. It is said that Egyptian peasants, innocent of any knowledge of squares on the hypotenuse being equal to the sum of squares on the remaining two sides of a triangle, became aware by observation that a triangular figure measuring, for example, 5 by 4 by 3 units gave them a right-angle from which progress to rectangle or a square was easy. Hence it was possible in very early times to parcel out strips of land. The many later niceties of surveying are beyond our present scope.

As to direction, we are accustomed to maps that have north at the top and south at the bottom. We say that this is how they are "orientated", using of course a word that indicates from west to east! There are indeed maps where east is at the top either because the principal religions came from Jerusalem and Mecca and the Far East, or for the more mundane later reason that the shape of the shire or island or country depicted conveniently fitted in the page in this fashion.

Since the route was initially of the first concern, variations in direction were of less importance. In plans of the Paris Metro and the London Underground distances and directions take second place to the succession of stations through which one must pass. Nor need scale be accurate. Thus primitive traders and soldiers and pilgrims required to know no more than the proper succession of landmarks and sea-marks.

In mapping, the big leap is upward and forward, from the man's-eye view of a land surface to the bird's-eye view. In some areas hills and mountains were there to give points of vantage, in others there was no visual-aid apart from the mind's-eye view. As late as the 16th century, Christopher Saxton's warrant indicated that facilities were to be granted to him "to be conducted unto any towre, castle, high place or hill to view the country".

Earlier maps are content to be frankly two-dimensional, indicating not very accurately length by breadth. The depth of the sea and height of the hills were first suggested pictorially. Uniform sea-depths were recorded first; land contour-lines followed.

Up to at least the second century before Christ the Greeks, who led geographical and all other scientific and quasi-scientific thought, imagined the world to be a flat disc surrounded by a vast sea under which the sun passed every night.

It was possible to begin with the concept of the Great Sea, the Mediterranean running east and west. This gave some kind of base line, but in the absence of direct knowledge and precise measurement too much emphasis was placed on the presumed Balance of Nature. This fancied symmetrical requirement led the earliest mappers to false conclusions that opposite coasts must curve similarly, that rivers must tend to run parallel, that islands corresponded to islands.

As realisation dawned that the Earth was curved and conviction grew that it was a globe, new problems arose for the mappers. Three-dimensional outlines had to be drawn as though they were two-dimensional. What came to be known as latitudinal references were in practice easier to record than longitudinal references. Variations in the altitude of the sun offered evidence of distance north or south from the Equator. Parallel lines of latitude numbered distances from the Equator to the North Pole while a similar set served from the Equator to the South Pole.

Following Ptolemy, early map makers visualised an initial meridian line of longitude through the Azores or the Canary Islands. John Seller moved to the base meridian of London in a map of 1676; John Cary initiated the use of the meridian of Greenwich in a map dated 1794; and there have been other prime meridians.

Since the Earth revolves full circle through 360 degrees in 24 hours, it must turn 15 degrees every hour. But to calculate the measurement on the Earth's surface of each degree of longitude required observation of astronomical movements and lunar eclipses and precise timing devices. The arrival and perfection of the magnetic compass facilitated the establishment of longitudinal location, especially when the difference between true and magnetic north could be evaluated.

The intersection of meridians of longitude and parallels of latitude cutting at right angles provides co-ordinates whereby any place can be identified. The navigator was now given the correct compass bearing of his course from point to point. This was essentially the achievement of Gerardus Mercator, the 16th century Flemish geographer. Mercator's famous projection is still in use. Eventually it has become possible to indicate with some precision on the Earth's surface the position, for example, of Newport, Gwent: latitude 51.35 degrees North, longitude 3 degrees West.

Whereas a globe flattened at top and bottom, an oblate spheroid, pretty accurately represents the Earth, a map however large involves distortion. The larger the area covered by the map, the greater is the tendency to distort unless one or other of many methods of geometrical and non-geometrical projections is used to reduce, but never wholly to eradicate, distortion. Fortunately, the size of a County is not great enough to warrant comparison and contrast of varying map projections.

However, even on County maps a smaller grid is useful. Arbitrary but not haphazard lines may be drawn vertically and horizontally and either lettered or numbered so that the square G3, for example, narrows a search for a location. A four-figure map reference obviously indicates a more precise spot. Thus the degree of sophistication in identifying locations is another criterion by which the age of a map may be gauged.

Maps are printed chronologically by three main methods: relief, intaglio, lithographic. The relief process involved drawing the map in ink as a mirror image on a wooden block and leaving the engraver to cut out the uninked wood, thus leaving a raised design. The intalgio (cutting-in) process by contrast normally involved incising the mirror-image map in a copper plate with a tool called a burin and inking the resulting furrows. Steel replaced copper in the 19th century. In both instances, paper under considerable pressure took the image of the intended map, less distinctly of course as the original wooden block or metal plate became worn with age and usage. Most of the maps listed in this book result from the original design having been cut on a metal plate.

In the 19th century, from about 1826, the new lithographic process involved drawing the design with a greasy pencil on a suitably prepared stone (in Greek 'lithos'). Damp paper under pressure again satisfies the printing requirement since grease and water do not mix.

There should be evidence beyond the edges of the map proper of the extent of the plate printed under pressure. This is why we still speak of a book's first or subsequent impression. Sometimes cropping removes the indentation; sometimes the indentation is a recent contrivance. Where a large map comes from an atlas there is likely to be a centre fold, but alas this too is easy to simulate in a reproduction.

As with all alleged antiques, the buyer of maps must be especially aware. If the paper is very white and smooth, the map is unlikely to be old. Up to the last quarter of the 18th century, it was the practice when sheets of paper were being made to allow them to dry in trays supported on parallel lines of wire. If the map be held up to a strong light, the parallel marks of these wires should appear. In addition there was often a water-mark of special design to each large sheet of paper, but that water-mark could possibly lie beyond the map-area cut to fit into an atlas.

Early maps were not easy to colour because early paper tended to be absorbent. Hand-colouring was not uncommon but, except for hundred boundaries and sometimes the hundreds themselves, it was usually added only at the request of the purchaser. Customers generally preferred to take plain maps to professional colourists. Occasionally the engraver gave the illuminator an indication, especially where coats-of-arms were included, of the appropriate colouring either by the form of hatching or shading or by a letter-key, as O for 'or' (gold) and A for argent (silver). Conventional colours were blue for water, green for woodland, brown for hills. The colour-printing of maps did not begin until the mid-nineteenth century.

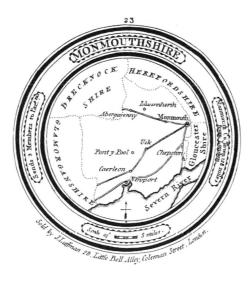

John Luffman, 1803

George Bickham's Panoramic View of the County (page 45)

CHAPTER II

The Making of a County

Small groups of Stone Age men and women wandered north into Britain when it was still joined to the Continent of Europe and the mammoth and hyena roamed in search of lesser prey. They hunted and fished and ate berries and insects at a venture. As primitive as New Guinea savages or Australian aborigines, they used caves and such other natural shelter as they could find.

New Stone Age men who found their way into South Wales before 2000 B.C. had some knowledge of food-production and of pottery. Though few traces of their habitations remain, they were the first home-builders. They have bequeathed to us their standing stones and megalithic burial chambers, with and without the covering of long earth barrows or cairns. Later arrivals came in search not only of sustenance, but also of tin and of copper, components that were to designate the Bronze Age. The Beaker Folk, so named from their distinctive potted cups, buried their dead not in long but in round earth barrows or under stone cairns on hill-tops.

The sites of their graves are ironically the principal reminders of the lives of long generations of scattered inhabitants of these islands whom we may conveniently call pre-Celtic. In what was to become Monmouthshire the evidence of pre-Celtic occupation is scanty. Though megalithic culture was widely spread in West Wales, here no more than three New Stone Age chambered tombs are known: Newchurch, Gwern-y-Cleppa, Heston Brake near Portskewett.

The comparative absence of archaeological finds in the County before the Iron Age suggests that the earliest colonists came, not overland through England, but by sea from the Continent direct or via Ireland or Devon and Cornwall. Of those who came ashore in South West Wales, few penetrated as far east as Monmouthshire/Gwent. The heavy alluvial plains, thickly wooded interior and deep valleys held little attraction for the earliest hunters and agriculturists.

There is archaeological evidence to indicate the broad movements of the Iron Age Celts from their cradle in Central Europe during the 4th and 3rd centuries B.C. Some travelled south towards the Mediterranean, some west into France and thence not only into Brittany, Cornwall, Ireland, Cumbria and Cambria. Significantly it was on the western sea-boards that they were to have an abiding influence, but the Celts penetrated into all parts of the British Isles. They were the first Britishers; they spoke a British tongue or tongues. The Celts who spread over most of the mainland of Britain spoke Brythonic, the forerunner of Welsh; the Celts who occupied Scotland and Ireland used the Goidelic form of Celtic, evolving into Gaelic and Erse and Manx.

With the Celts we meet for the first time one tribe, the Silures, associated principally though not entirely with the eventual Monmouthshire. There were successive waves of Celts bringing with them a variety of cultures, broadly divided by archaeologists into Iron Age A, B and C. The Celts were warriors armed with bronze and latterly iron weapons, easily able to subdue and even to enslave non-Celtic predecessors. The newcomers were generally tall and fair-headed. It has been fancifully suggested that the smaller dark, so-called Iberians overwhelmed by them became the Little People of Celtic legend, able as cave-and-hole-and-corner dwellers to appear and disappear speedily, mysterious and therefore magical.

Celtic tribes were extended families claiming common descent and presumably therefore having some common characteristics. The Silures for example, get a special mention in Tacitus for ferocity and tenacity, now in part sublimated by Rugby football.

Sixty separate local Gothic tribes were listed on one Roman monument in Gaul. Too little is known about the linguistic and other characteristics that distinguished even major tribes like the Silures who occupied an area in South-east Wales rather wider than the eventual County. There are references in other early historians to the Silures, but gone is the easy confidence with which former writers served a mish-mash of Celtic history from myth and legend and romanticised ancient literature.

How different were the Silures from the Demetae to the west and Ordovices, Venedotae, Deceangli et al. to the north? There is some hard evidence that they constructed their hill-forts differently. There must have been at least dialectal variations when we remind ourselves that in California alone 150 different "Red Indian" languages were spoken by immigrant tribes. It would be pleasant to think that Silurian druids officiated and Silurian bards sang hymns and arias in proto-Monmouthshire speech.

It has been pointed out that if life on earth began with the first living cell 3,000 million years ago then, scaling down that scarcely imaginable period to one calendar year, man would not appear until the evening of December 31st. Bemused by what seems to our short-sighted eyes to be the remote past, we forget that the Iron Age Celts, and among them the Silures, highly skilled in art and in crafts, had been in Britain perhaps 1000 years before the Romans came. Civilisations had risen and fallen in China, India, Egypt, Crete and Mycenae.

Julius Caesar's abortive invasions of Britain in 55 B.C. and 54 B.C. never permitted him to draw near enough to South-east Wales to meet the Silures at home. Another century was to elapse before there was a serious threat to Silurian domination.

Llanmelin above Caerwent was the principal stronghold of the Silurian tribe. There was an important military site at the Bulwarks, Chepstow, commanding a view of approaches from the sea and a river-crossing to the West of England, which was to continue to play a significant part in the subsequent history of the future County. There were numerous hill-top forts with simple or complex earth and stone defences from the Gaer at Newport to those above the valleys running north-west and north-east.

The Silurian administrative centre could have been Caerwent long before the Romans confirmed it as a civil settlement, Venta Silurum. The name Gwent occurring as an element in Caerwent signifies a trading-centre. In post-Roman times Caerwent was still known as Guentonie Urbs, the town of Gwent, but the pre-Roman appearance of the eventual name for Monmouthshire certainly does not imply a pre-Roman concept of a County area. In fact Gwent originally was only the eastern part of the County, a cantref in pre-Norman times divided into Gwent Iscoed and Uwchcoed, below and above the forest.

The full-scale Roman invasion of Britain began in 43 A.D. in the reign of the Emperor Claudius. Arriving in South Wales nearly 30 years after the initial Claudian landing in Kent, the grandsons and great-grandsons of Caesar's Romans finally established the 2nd Augustan Legionary fort at Isca (Caer Lleon, Castra Legionum) in 75 A.D. There was an earlier fort at Burrium, Usk. The Silures had put up strong resistance under Caratacus, or Caradog, a leader who was not a member of their tribe but a son of Cunobelinus, Shakespeare's Cymbeline, lately King of South-east Britain. Caratacus was captured and sent to Rome where he was heard to wonder why natives of that noble city wished to capture the hovels of the Celts, some of which he had seen in Monmouthshire.

The Romans knew the military value of good land and sea communications. From Caerleon to the other Legionary base at Chester lines of roads and forts were designed to penetrate and police what was to become Wales.

Venta Silurum (Caerwent) stood astride the main Roman road running west from Glevum (Gloucester) to Maridunum (Carmarthen). Within the incipient Monmouthshire area, roads would have linked Abergavenny (Gobannium), Burrium (Usk) and Blestium (Monmouth) with the coastal road, number XII in the ANTONINE ITINERARY, M4 to you and me. The Romans continued the use of the short passage across the river Severn near Caerwent. They may have strengthened the sea-walls that emphasised a natural southern boundary. They thinned forests and began the drainage of the soggy south.

There is, however, no evidence that the Romans thought of Wales as a separate country. They did not designate any sub-command approximating to a County within the wide area controlled from the Legionary fort at Caerleon. Monmouthshire was in no sense a Romano-British entity. The establishment with headquarters at Caerwent of a respublica civitatis Silurum, a commonwealth of the state of the Silures, was as far as Rome was prepared to go. The Roman policy was to conquer first by division and secondly by Romanisation. The Romans were ready to grant the Silures some autonomy once Silurian culture, religion and secular institutions were sufficiently Romanised.

British soldiers served in the so-called Army along with troops and auxiliaries from all over the Empire, but no separate cohort was raised from the Silures as from other tribes. Nevertheless, Celticisation overtook Romanisation. By the end of the 2nd century A.D. it became impossible in Roman Britain to distinguish between 'the Romans' and the Britons.

To the West the tribes, including the Silures, retained their language which evolved into primitive

22

Welsh. For legal and administrative purposes only, colloquial Celtic, assimilating a large Latin vocabulary, gave way to Latin. Later the partner languages were Welsh and Norman-French, later still Welsh and English. In England, of course, Anglo-Saxon ultimately ousted Celtic except in a considerable number of place-names some of which may indeed be pre-Celtic.

Defence of the Roman province of Britain began to crumble towards the end of the 3rd century A.D. The island was virtually defenceless before the end of the 4th century A.D. Not much trust is now placed in a set date 450 A.D. for the coming of the Saxons. There is evidence that Germanic soldiers in large numbers were employed by the Romano-British to keep out other Germanic tribesmen who finally overwhelmed them. A long racial overlap would help to explain why the British tongue was no longer to be heard in England. Certainly all the Celts could not have fled to Wales: the British did not abandon their country to the English. Celtic warriors and peaceful settlers from Scotland and from Ireland swarmed into West and North Wales. Pagan Saxons threatened from the east the patchily Christianised Silures.

Christianity was adopted as the official religion of the Roman Empire under Constantine in 312 A.D. There is a chi-rho, the first two letters of Christ's name in Greek, scratched on a Caerwent pewter pot belonging probably to the 4th century. The groundwork of the Caerwent basilica may be Christian. From the 5th century there took place the first great Welsh Religious Revival as the Saints came marching in from Gaul, from Ireland, from the Mediterranean.

The connection of King Arthur with Caerleon, despite the fantasies of Giraldus Cambrensis and others, is legend rather than history. But either Arthur or Ambrosius Aurelianus, the latter being something more than a legend, held up the Germanic invaders at the battle of Mons Badonicus early in the 6th century. This was an important factor in preserving the Celtic character of the West of Britain when elsewhere the British were rapidly losing their language and becoming increasingly English and Saxon, Anglo-Saxon. No one now accepts the story that invaders drove all the Celts of Britain west.

South-east Wales was very vulnerable to the Danish attacks which culminated here in the 10th century. However, the invading foreigners may have assisted the process of unification in Wales.

Of course, the early post-Roman Welsh princes themselves had territorial aspirations. Regional names in West and North Wales lend credence to the story of the rise of the dynasty of Cunedda, a Celt from Scotland, since several regions echo the names of Cunedda's sons.

In South-east Wales sometime in the 5th century there appears Glywys, King of Glywysing. He and his family controlled loosely the former Glamorgan and part of Monmouthshire, their lands stretching West from the Usk to the Towy.

Gwynllyw, father of Cadoc, inherited that part of Glywysing between the Usk and the Rhymney rivers. Gwynllyw was anglicised as St Woolo; his territory became known as Wentloog. But Wentloog (Gwynllwg) strangely has no direct etymological connection with Gwent, originally a separate princedom which lay to the east of the Usk. It was to be combined at a much later date with Wentloog.

By the 8th century the Mercian King Offa's Dyke indicated a crude Wales—England division which did not wholly accord with linguistic differences. Some later Norman Lordships stood astride the Dyke which served, however, to indicate the eventual eastern limit of Monmouthshire. Mountains and rivers and the sea circumscribed the rest of the developing shire, or a shire ripe for development.

Two kinds of ecclesiastical establishments had some influence on the localisation of territories; monastic institutions and smaller congregations under priests. Caerwent is an example of a monastic church said to have been run by a community or "clas" of clerical canons under a superior not necessarily ordained. Theodore of Tarsus, Archbishop of Canterbury in the late 7th century, laid the foundations of ecclesiastical boundaries, but dioceses, deaneries, parishes were not clearly defined until after the tidy-minded Normans arrived. The early Bishops were spiritual not temporal leaders; monks and friars attached more importance to preaching and prayer than to pastoral administration within a given area.

The Normans found no difficulty in merging into a feudal, manorial system the ecclesiastical networks such as they were. The feudal lord at least in theory himself owed his lordship through the King to the King of Kings.

The Normans arriving in South Wales found what was to be Monmouthshire divided like Caesar's Gaul into three parts or cantrefs. The area was split vertically into Gwynllwg and Gwent, the latter being divided horizontally into Uwchcoed (Upper Gwent) and Iscoed (Netherwent), above and below Wentwood. Upper and Lower Gwent were separate cantrefs (groups literally of a hundred communities). Smaller still were commotes, convenient administrative districts; an instance was the commote of Erging or Archenfield, to be largely lost to Herefordshire later.

The Normans carved among themselves the Marches, that part of Wales that "marched" alongside England. Norman families in Norman castles parcelled Gwynllwg and Gwent into their lordships more effectively than any previous secular or religious intruders. Civil and ecclesiastical boundaries largely coincided. Anomalies, where they occurred, are unusual and of special interest. Provided that feudal dues were paid to the appropriate lordship, isolated and outlying pockets of people could preserve their own language and customs in Welshries.

Clockwise, there were the lordship divisions of Gwynllwg (Wentloog); Bergavenny; Grosmont; White Castle; Skenfrith; Monmouth; Trelech; Strigoil (Chepstow); Caerleon; Usk. The sub-lordships of Raglan and Caldicot grew in importance later. At Mathern and Goldcliff there were ecclesiastical lordships. At this early date we can already see dimly ahead to the seven Hundreds, familiar from the printed maps.

The separation of Wales from England became more marked under the Normans. It is significant that William the Conqueror ordered in the Domesday book of 1086 A.D. a survey of all lands of England, not England and Wales. There are for this reason few references to Monmouthshire locations and those chiefly to the east of the Usk. The lordship of Caldicot, for example, is mentioned because it was held by the Sheriff of Gloucester. The Sheriff is the Shire-reeve. Both elements of the words are Old English and pre-Norman. The Shire existed in England but not in Wales before 1066. The Normans preferred the name County, derived from French.

Edward I demanded homage from Wales. Although this led to the Wars of Welsh Independence ending with the death of Llywelyn, the last native Prince of Wales, in 1282, the ensuing centralisation of royal power further hastened the rationalisation of local administrative and judicial government elsewhere in Wales. Gradually the Crown became a big land-owner in South-east Wales. Crown lands held by the Duchy of Lancaster were practically coterminous with the old Lordship of Monmouth. When the last of the Clares in the male line was killed at Bannockburn in 1314, extensive estates in the region became the gift of the Crown. In 1400, Owain Glyndwr was ostensibly leading the Welsh against the King of England, though this did not inhibit him from destroying Norman/Welsh towns including Newport.

During the Wars of the Roses Monmouthshire, like the rest of Wales, was divided in allegiance between Yorkists and Lancastrians. The Middle Ages ended in 1485 at Bosworth. Henry VII of Welsh ancestry, the first of the Tudor monarchs, came to the English Throne and the path to the Act of Union in the next century was cleared.

The Act of 1536 abolished all the formerly autonomous Marcher Lordships. All Wales, including what was later to become Monmouthshire, was divided into thirteen Counties. Gwynllwg and Gwent were finally united under the name taken from the royal lordship of Monmouth. Representatives of parishes, hundreds and the county, elected by limited franchise or simply appointed, exercised control where for centuries tribal chiefs, Roman officers, Welsh princes and Norman lords had held sway.

The anomalous position of Monmouthshire following the Act of Union of 1536 conferred certain unlooked-for benefits. Doubt as to whether Monmouthshire was in Wales or in England gave Newport rugby players a dual international qualification. Also, there are more maps of Monmouthshire than of any other Welsh county since it also invariably appeared in sets of maps of English Counties!

Monmouthshire legally ceased to be uneasily tacked on as "Wales and Monmouthshire" in 1968. The Act of 1974 added to it a couple of parishes from the former Breconshire and deducted a few for Mid-Glamorgan. The County now resumed the old territorial title of Gwent. What was the name of part became the name of the whole. Since 1974, Gwent is unlikely to change its boundaries again in the foreseeable future and it is without any doubt in Wales.

24

The Arms of Monmouth

CHAPTER III

Mapping before Saxton

The pioneer work of W.G. Hoskins promoted interest in the interaction between landscape and history. Aerial photography has revealed more of the habitations and activities of prehistoric and historic peoples. Landscape studies have given us a better idea of what lost or undrawn maps of the pre-Christian and early Christian era would have looked like. For example, Professor Hoskins has shown that down the centuries in Britain up to 3,000 villages, some of them never identified in maps, have ceased to exist or have been moved elsewhere for social, economic, military or health reasons.

The relevant geographical features, the manuscript and printed maps and extant plans are being re-examined as hitherto neglected ancillaries to the history of the decline and fall of Roman Britain, the 16th century Dissolution of the Monasteries, the 18th century Enclosure Acts, the 19th century Industrial Revolution.

Hypothetics has been defined as the science of that which might have happened, but did not. The cartographical branch of this science consists in the drawing of maps which should have been drawn, but were not. Their modern descendants have attempted to fill the gaps left by remote ancestors who had no mapping lore.

In PREHISTORIC AND EARLY WALES (1965), edited by Idris Foster and Glyn Daniel, one may find credible distribution maps of the Neolithic settlement in Wales, though there are but few round and long mounds between the Rhymney and the Wye. In the later phases of the Bronze and Iron Ages, an increasing number of tribal hill-forts appear in Monmouthshire/Gwent. In the Romano-British period very many sites may be plotted with tolerable accuracy. Very much earlier, Cyril Fox in his PERSONALITY OF BRITAIN (1932) had been able to reconstruct from archaeological evidence route-ways over land and sea.

More ambitiously in 1923 with a map of England and Wales in Roman times at the 1:1,250,000 scale, O.G.S. Crawford of the Ordnance Survey initiated what was to become a useful and dependable series of reconstructions. Within 20 years, there were attractive Ordnance Survey maps, not only of Roman Britain, but of Neolithic South Wales and of Britain in the Dark Ages. Maps of putative Ancient Britain, Monastic Britain and of Southern Britain in the Iron Age arrived after the second World War.

Locally, the Iron Age map, for example, indicates hill-forts and similarly defended enclosures: Twm Barlwm, Tredegar Camp (the Gaer Fort at Newport), Lodge Wood Camp (above Caerleon), Llanmelin Wood (above Caerwent), Wilcrick Hill, Piercefield Great Camp and a few other sites between the Usk and Wye.

In historical times written evidence, not only in the classical languages, places retrospective mapping upon firmer ground. Before 200 B.C., Pytheas, a Greek of Marseilles, wrote an account of a visit to the western coasts of Europe which admittedly is known only through Strabo who threw some doubts on the earlier narrative.

The Romans were chiefly interested in routes rather than the country through which their bee-line roads ran. Reluctant mariners, they clung as far as possible to land, throwing frequent bridges, as students of Caesar will recall, across inconvenient rivers.

Copies of Roman itineraries and geographical descriptions by Pliny and other classical writers survive. Julius Caesar in his CONQUEST OF GAUL describes, not without inaccuracy, the shape of Britain. *The Island is triangular, with one side facing Gaul. One corner ... points east ... (one) corner points south ... Another side faces west towards Spain.* Pomponius Mela, a geographer who was a native of Spain, up-dates knowledge of Britain for the Claudian invasion of 43 A.D. However, Tacitus, whose father-in-law Agricola was Governor of Britain, was still asserting towards the end of the first century A.D., that Ireland lay between Wales and Spain. He could and should have known better, but chaps interested him more than maps.

We read of the Roman map of the world associated with the name of Agrippa, son-in-law of the Emperor Augustus, said to have been completed before the Birth of Christ. It is probable that smaller copies of this official ORBIS TERRARUM were circulated within the Roman Empire. No doubt later versions included the Imperial expansions. The Agrippa map probably provided the basis for a chain of maps leading ultimately to the mediaeval Mappae Mundi, maps of the world, like the celebrated example on vellum in Hereford Cathedral, dated between 1280 and 1300 A.D.

Of course map-making had not ceased during the Dark Ages upon which so much more light has been shed recently. We shall not recover them, but countless crude maps, plans and charts must have been devised by Celt and Norseman, Saxon and Norman. Shakespeare's legendary King Lear's call for a map of Britain to divide his kingdom into three parts for his daughters need not be dismissed as an anachronism. The Norman DOMESDAY BOOK provides excellent resource material for a map of William's Conquest. Gerald the Welshman's ITINERARY THROUGH WALES made in 1188 is geographically sketchy and unsound.

Matthew Paris's map of Great Britain drawn about 1250 A.D. and the rather later Bodleian Gough map, probably of the 14th century, show an unshapely Wales. There is little of note apart from Snowdon, but at least Wales has a recognised place in the larger world. In hypothesis, however, locations can and have been entered on the map of Wales long before Saxton. Mediaeval pilgrims could not have lacked written information about routes to St David's, Canterbury or Rome, to which if all roads ran some were much to be preferred!

William Rees has bequeathed to us a set of four detailed, reconstructed maps of South Wales and the Border in the 14th century. On a scale of half-an-inch to the mile, he has indicated the domains of the Marcher Lords and the major territorial units within those domains. In what is now Gwent the principal divisions are Gwynllwg, Caerleon, Strigoil (Chepstow and Caldecote and Newton), Bergavenny, Monmouth (including the triangle of Grosemont, Skenfrith, White Castle). Newportonians will easily recognise Malum Passum (Malpas), Crinde (Crindau) and Stowe (at the top of Stow Hill). Natives of Pontypool may be surprised to find that Le Pool in the 14th century appears not to have been in the front row of towns and to have been of less importance than Mamylad and Pen Pelleni (sic) where there were mesne lordships or sub-lordships.

As early as the second century A.D., Ptolemy had put together in his GEOGRAPHIA material for maps of the then known World. His work was lost and forgotten for centuries. It was not until 1475 A.D. that a Latin edition of Ptolemy finally brought cartography once again out of the mists of myth and legend. Wales makes an appearance in the reconstructed Ptolemy world-map in its proper place to the west of England, though Scotland is bent eastwards askew from the north of England. For two or three hundred years, most maps were to be founded upon or influenced by the long-forgotten resurrected work of Ptolemy.

Plagiarism has not always been considered reprehensible. In post-classical literature, the inclusion of an elegant extract from an earlier model, copied or imitated, was regarded as a praiseworthy achievement. Similarly in mapping, cartographers paid tribute to distinguished predecessors by incorporating their work rather than looking afresh at the country to be mapped. *Drawn from an original survey* does not necessarily mean *drawn from a new survey*.

We have to wait until the 16th century before there are printed and manuscript maps in which a recognisably accurate outline of Wales appears. Gerhard Mercator, the Flemish geographer, born in 1512, combined extensive theoretical knowledge with great practical ability. He was not only a gifted surveyor and engraver, but he made mathematical instruments. Mercator corrected earlier distortions and errors; his new projection allowed for the convergence of the meridians on the globe and yet represented them as straight lines of latitude and longitude on a flat map. Mercator did more than correct Ptolemy; he made a new start, not least because he had new instrumental means but because he saw that allowances must be made for magnetic variation. Ptolemy's work continued however to influence traditionally conservative marine navigators.

The earliest sea-charts and portolanos giving sailing directions in the 14th and 15th centuries were constructed with the aid of the first crude mariners' compasses. For our particular purpose it is interesting to note that the coastal outline from the English Channel around the South coast of England to the estuary of the Thames is charted with reasonable accuracy early in the 14th century. The fact that continental traders were sailing in the Bristol Channel gives us a very early outline of Monmouthshire's coastline. This was a century before Christopher Columbus sailed chartless into the Atlantic to arrive in 1493 in the West Indies, which he took to be the East Indies.

After Mercator, c.1564 A.D., and Laurence Howell, also in the 1560's, Humphrey Llwyd, a Denbighshire scholar, supplied the data for the first credible maps of England and Wales and separately of Wales. These were published by Ortelius in Antwerp in 1573 in an enlarged edition of his 1570 THEATRUM ORBIS TERRARUM. Humphrey Llwyd himself died before the maps were issued, but they bear his name.

The Llwyd map of Wales names places sometimes not only in Latin but also in Welsh (which he calls British) and in English (Anglo-Saxon). Although there is no demarcation line drawn, Gwent/Siluria on the map may be taken to coincide broadly with the later Monmouthshire, now returned to its earlier name, Gwent.

Gwent is intersected from west to east by diagrammatic rivers: Rhymney, Usk, Wye and Severn — the Monnow is the only tributary mentioned.

The sparse named places are:

Abergefenni
Caerleon/Civitas legionum
Caer Went/Venta Silurum
Caldicot
Castelth Gwent/Strigulia/Chepstowe
Castle Newydh/Newport
Goldcliffe
Magur
Nash
Raglan
Skinfreth
Tredegyr (Tredegar Park, Newport)
Usk

We can, of course, check maps and charts from cross-references in literary and other documents. But we should remember that lazy cartographers could also have found books more accessible, if less dependable, than the land they purported to map.

John Leland was appointed King's Antiquary by Henry VIII and visited Wales between 1536 and 1539. It will be remembered that this was soon after the Dissolution of the Monasteries (1534-35) and the Act of Union (1535-36). Unfortunately Leland's ITINERARY has disappointingly little to say about Monmouthshire at a crucial point in its history. He does refer to the Llantarnam Abbey of White Monks *lately suppressed*. However, Leland's detailed description of the sites of the triangle of castles, Skenfrith, Grosmont and White Castle, may have saved the feet of later surveyors.

There are discrepancies between Leland and Saxton. Leland says, *there is a stone bridge over Monnow a little* above *the Castle* (of Skenfrith). Saxton's bridge is clearly drawn *below* the Castle. Before 1540, Leland described *the causey or high-way ... from Newport to Pont Remney, crossing the Ebbw at Bassaleg.* This is useful knowledge because Saxton does not include this or other roads. Leland is not always an eye-witness: *Porteskewin* (Portskewett), as I learned, *is betwixt Chepstow and Cairguent* (Caerwent)!

Leland gives an account of the older house of the Morgans of South Wales *on the farther ripe* (or bank) *of Elboith* (Ebbw) *ryver in Wentllugh. It is called Tredeger,* he reports, *nother castle or pile, but a maner* (manor) *place.* His estimate of its distance from Newport *within a mile* is plainly wrong.

For our part of the world the prosaic verse of Thomas Churchyard's THE WORTHINES OF WALES (1587) is not without interest. It supplements cartography and may again have been plundered by cartographers.

Behind Wentwood in a clump of trees only a few stones remain of Saxton's Strogle Castle. Evidently it was pretty dilapidated even in Churchyard's day. He versifies Stroge Castle, as he spells it:

... upon a side, of woody hill full fair,
This castle stands, full sore decayed and broke,
Yet builded once, in fresh and wholesome air,
Full near great woods, and many a mighty oak ...

The location is imprecisely described and, when Churchyard continues in the next but one stanza, he is even less reliable:

Two myles from that, upon a mightie hill,
Langibby stands, a castle once of state

In 1612 and 1622, Michael Drayton published in two parts his POLYOLBION accompanied by quaint regional "maps". The poet travelled widely in England and Wales gathering material. He borrowed books and advice from the prominent antiquarians of his day, John Selden, John Stow and William Camden.

There is nothing quite as extensive as Drayton's work until Daniel Defoe's TOUR THROUGH GREAT BRITAIN (1724), by which date there were already at least twenty five different maps of Monmouthshire, including road maps.

Towards the end of the 18th century, maps became indispensable as travellers poured into Wales, usually beginning their journey in Monmouthshire. Many were equipped with both pen and pencil and the numerous books which they wrote are illustrated, often with maps.

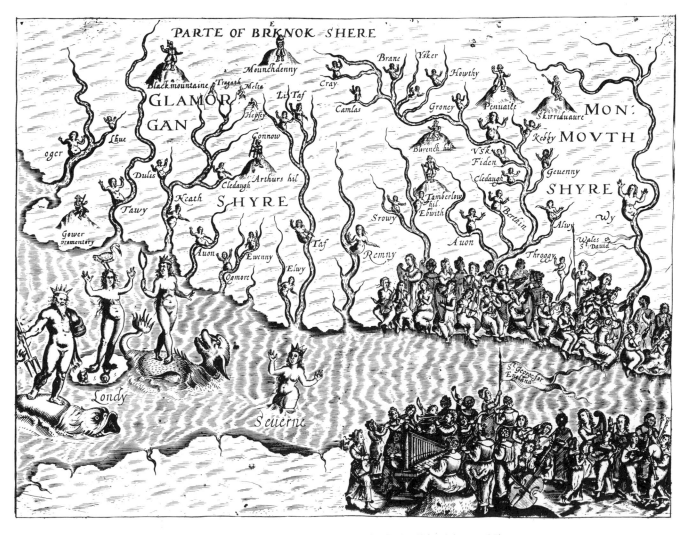

Illustration from Michael Drayton's 'Polyolbion' (page 37)

CHAPTER IV

The Naming of Monmouthshire

Monmouthshire's lines of communication with the rest of Wales have always been more difficult than those overland with Gloucestershire and Herefordshire and those across the Bristol Channel with South-west England. English influence has been more potent than in any other Welsh county, with the exception of Radnorshire.

Yet Welsh place-names survive in great numbers, although mispronunciation, misspelling and the passage of time have conspired to disfigure them. Not the least diverting example is the elucidation by the historian, E.T. Davies, from a Llangybi estate document, of the field-name Cape of Scotland! It started as Cae Pysgodlyn, the Field of the Fishpool.

Not every Celtic-looking place-name is genuinely antique. The Welsh prefix *Llan* relates to a church foundation and usually introduces the name of the saint or founder to whom the church was dedicated. Llan seems first to have been applied to an enclosure and then to the land on which stood a monastic institution, large or small. Later, the Llan appears to have indicated the enclosure wherein was a church or chapel, perhaps established by a monk. But we are not to assume that Llanover took its name from a church dedicated to St Gofor, for such a saint never existed. (G)ofor/Over was possibly the invention of Lady Llanover, wife of Lord Llanover the Big Ben who gave *his* name to a famous clock, though Professor Gwynedd Pierce has proposed St Mofor.

The name Bassaleg is an interesting example of the danger of making an easy assumption about the derivation of a place-name. Bassaleg may look sufficiently Celtic, but it is of Greek derivation. The Greek word *basileus* means a king; some early churches were built on the plan of a royal or *basilican* palace, a rectangle with a semi-circular apse at one end. There must have been an early basilica where the river Ebbw could first be easily forded and bridged. At a later date, the church was dedicated to St Basil, when the true derivation of its name had already been forgotten. It is fortuitous that the Christian name Basil derives from the same Greek kingly root. It is clearly vain to search for a Celtic original, such as Maes Helyg, the field of the willows, or the Maes of some dubious Alectus. Greek is not a source we would expect to find among Monmouthshire names.

Place-names present a linguistic mine-field into which we venture at our peril, even when we follow the footsteps of expert toponymists. The wisest scholars have proceeded with the greatest caution.

It is true that Margaret Gelling was writing about the place-names of England, but it is useful to recall that, in SIGNPOSTS TO THE PAST (1978), she distinguished between six principal linguistic sources: pre-Celtic, Celtic, Latin, Old English, Scandinavian, Norman-French. In very different proportions, the same six sources apply to Monmouthshire (Gwent).

First, there was an unknown pre-Celtic, non-Indo-European language, elements of which may have survived in river names. In this county, for example, Usk, especially in view of its occurrence elsewhere in Britain in many forms, as Exe, Axe, Esk, not to mention the first syllable of whisk-ey (water-of-life), may echo indistinctly a pre-Celtic word for water.

Forms of pre-Celtic and subsequently of Celtic were spoken throughout these islands. Throughout Britain, but especially in Wales, there is an extensive legacy of "British", that is to say Celtic, place-names. A glance at Monmouthshire maps, old and new, shows the persistence of Welsh place-names, like the Welsh language itself, particularly in the rural areas and in the hilly north of the county, rather than in the anglicised south.

Anglicisation came late and slowly. The Act of Union of 1536 established a somewhat artificial boundary. There were both Welsh and English speakers who found themselves on the wrong side of the arbitrary border. In Erging, or Archenfield, in south-west Herefordshire Welsh inhabitants had little choice but to succumb to English speech. But not immediately. In the late 16th century the Bishop of Hereford still had to provide Welsh Bibles and Prayer-books for some parishes in his diocese.

In parts of Radnorshire the English-speakers, caught west of the border, took less easily to the new-old Welsh language.

Welsh was wide-spread in Monmouthshire up to the latter half of the 18th century, but it began to lose ground in the 19th century with the quick growth in an immigrant population. Of course, among these were many Welsh-speakers, especially from Carmarthenshire and Cardiganshire, but they did not all encourage their children and grand-children to keep their native language.

Even into the 20th century, there were high percentages of Welsh-speakers in Rhymney according to the Census Returns: 68.9% in 1901; 55.9% in 1911; 46.5% in 1921; 44.4% in 1931; thereafter, dropping to 12% in 1971. In 1901, one in eight Monmouthshire dwellers still spoke Welsh.

Significantly, Archdeacon William Coxe in his HISTORICAL TOUR OF MONMOUTHSHIRE (1801) refers to the value of an interpreter, the Reverend Mr Evans, vicar of St Woolos: *I scarcely made a single excursion in the vicinity of Newport in which I was not accompanied by Mr Evans, and derived the greatest advantage from his knowledge of the Welsh tongue.*

We must add more than a pinch of salt to George Borrow's statement in the penultimate chapter of WILD WALES (1862): *I believe the real fact is that about half the people for seven or eight miles to the* east *of Newport speak Welsh more or less, as about half of those whom I met and addressed in Welsh answered me in that tongue.* There are still plenty of *Bore da* Welshmen about, not only in Gwent.

We shall return to the subject of the Welshness of Monmouthshire. But what was the linguistic effect of the Roman invasion of Britain in the first century A.D.? Surprisingly little. Of course there are many Latin words in Welsh to this day from the vocabulary of building and weaponry, of medicine and elementary science, but it is remarkable that comparatively few place-names were latinised during a couple of centuries of occupation. After all, the Romans bequeathed to occupied France and Spain and Portugal native versions of Latin, ousting existing languages.

Just as it was Roman policy to romanise local deities, so also it seems to have been Roman policy, at least in this part of Britain, where possible merely to latinise previous place-names. Isca is clearly from Usk, not vice versa. Many place-names have been identified from the ANTONINE ITINERARY of the first century A.D. Gobannium is from the British word for a blacksmith and is translated or re-translated eventually into (Aber)gavenny. Burrium, the Roman fort at Usk, and Blestium, the Romano-British settlement at Monmouth, may arise from personal names.

There are pitfalls in looking too assiduously for Roman influence. Malpas, a difficult passage, seems to be directly from the latin. But the name is not recorded until 1291 A.D. It was so named, not by the Romans, but by the Normans.

The fourth linguistic source, Anglo-Saxon or Old English, is the most productive and yet the most perplexing in its operation. The "British" or Celtic tongue was spoken not simply in Wales but generally throughout Britain before the English arrived. The newcomers could hardly have enslaved and de-nationed all the Celts in England or driven the survivors west, as was once supposed. Why did the new invaders impose their own language so thoroughly when the Romans had not succeeded, if indeed they tried?

It has been suggested that the crude date A.D. 450 for the *Adventus Saxonum* (the coming of the Saxons) is mis-leading. Perhaps there was a long, slow process of infiltration. Perhaps continental Germanic troops were widely employed by the Romans. Perhaps they settled in Roman-Britain long before the Romans left — and there is ceramic evidence to support this view. We have too readily accepted the concept of Roman-Britain; we ought to have paid more attention to the idea of Romano-England.

Whatever happened to the Celtic vernacular, the old names of places were least affected everywhere. Eighteen rivers and streams are named by Saxton on his Monmouthshire map of 1577. Most of them bear Welsh, or fractured-Welsh names: e.g. Sroway; Ebwith; Kebby (Cibi); Birthin; Trothy; Throggy; Rompney (Rhymni); Cledagh, a name found in various forms all over Wales. Sabrina is the name given by the Romans to the Severn, in Welsh Hafren. The standard work on Welsh river-names is ENWAU AFONYDD A NANTYDD CYMRU by R.J. Thomas.

On the other hand, the river-names Wye and perhaps Olwye (Olway) may be English. There are grounds for believing that these two belong to a large group of names built on the Old English element weoh, wih, meaning heathen shrine. Compare Patchway, Wyham, Wyville, Weoley, Willey, Weedon. Mynwy, the Welsh form of the river Monnow, appears to describe it as the Little Wye.

There is no argument about the Englishness of Chepstow, a market-place. Compare Cheap as in Cheapside and Chippenham and Stow, as at Wonastow and Dingestow and everywhere else in Britain. Newport, Marshfield, Nash (remove the initial letter to reveal the ash tree) and Caldicot (cold cottages) are very un-Welsh names. More modern settlements like Sebastopol and Markham are named from the battle and a collier owner!

Tun is Old English for a farmstead or village, the nucleus often of a later town. Saxton offers us in Monmouthshire Byssheton, Dewston, Dixton, Ifton, Langston, Mounton, Peterston, Rochesten, Runston, Stanton, Wolfenewton, Wytston. Clearly, several of those names ending in -ston described stones, no -tuns. It is absurd to imagine a farmstead or village for example on Saxton's Charston rock.

If we accept that -wick is English, but derived from Latin *vicus*, as is now confidently proposed for place-names in England, we shall find ourselves in difficulties in Monmouthshire. It is not easy to visualise Roman occupation links with Howick or Redwick.

The fifth linguistic source mentioned above results from the Scandinavian invasions. We have few Old Norse place-name elements like -by and -thorpe, so common on the east coasts of England. Only -holm in the Steep- and Flat-Holms betrays temporary incursions of the Danes before the Normans came.

We turn to the sixth and the last linguistic influence, Norman-French. It is odd that the Normans, the North men, lost their Scandinavian tongue when they moved into Northern France. It is odder still that having adapted French, or their version of it, they appear to have made no effort to impose the language generally on the conquered English and Welsh. They were content to conduct legal and other business in it. They left the thinnest deposit of Norman-French place-names in the county.

There is Grismond (Grosmont) which defines itself as a large mound. There is Rockefeld (Rockfield) derived not very obviously from Rocheville. Goldcliff is an example of a place-name that certainly ought to have become French since the alien Priory at Goldcliff was a dependent of the Norman abbey of Bec-Hellouin and had French priors throughout its history from the 12th to the 15th century. Gerald the Welshman, writing in about 1188 A.D., says that Goldcliff was named from its appearance from the Channel; he adds that other derivations are possible and recommends digging there for gold or for oil, *oleum de saxo!*

The principal linguistic effect of the arrival of the Normans was upon the pronunciation and therefore upon the spelling of existing names, uncertain though this remained for centuries. Gallic difficulties, observable to this day, with -CH- and with -TH- meant that these tended to become -C- and -T-. The -chesters became -cesters. The Throggy Brook became the Troggy. Trothy became Troy.

Topographically through all these comings and goings Monmouthshire remained stubbornly Welsh. The commonest inspiration for place-names came from Celtic Christianity. Traditionally, St Cadoc, head of the great religious house at Llancarfan, Glamorgan, is reputed to have been a native of Llangattock-nigh-Usk. Hence four village-names in the Vale of Usk embed his name.

Saxton has no fewer than forty Monmouthshire place-names beginning with Lan-, Lann-, Llan-, and Llann-. Many celebrate saints either forgotten or not easily identified. Allowance for mutation reveals Llanbadoc as the church of St Madoc; the several Llanddewi's were St David's; Llandegveth was St Tegfedd's; Llanelen, St Helen's; Llantrissent was shared by three saints, Peter, Paul and John. It is not easy to spot St Oudoceus at Llandogo or St Illtyd at Llanhilleth. Nor is it easy to extract St Mabli from Llanvapley.

It may be significant that, in the reign of Elizabeth, Saxton records only one Mary dedication, that at Llanvaier Kilgeden! Did the Virgin Mary have to pay for the unpopularity of the former Queen? It ought to be noted that dedications changed for reasons not always now explicable.

It does not follow that Welsh and English have the same names for the same places. The best known example here of a difference in appellation is Newport which in Welsh is known as Casnewydd (Newcastle). At Chepstow also the Welsh note the castle and know the town as Cas Gwent.

There remain many anomalies and curiosities. There are hybrid place-names, part-English, part-Welsh, like Dewston where Dewi is associated with an English stone. Penhow has a Welsh top to an English or Old Norse hill! Wonastow and Dingestow have home-grown saints, Winwaloe and Dingad, in English -stows.

Occasionally English seems to precede Welsh. Saxton and later cartographers record Grenefeld Castle, now a mere mound in Maesglas, its direct Welsh translation. Nor can English names always be taken at their face value: there were no wolves at Wolvesnewton — Ralph le Wolf held the manor in 1314. The very English-sounding Skenfrith disguises Ynys-Cynfraeth.

Names suffer curious land-changes. St Treacle chapel on Treacle Rock in the Severn was dedicated probably to St Tecla and was originally sited on a peninsula that became an island. By contrast, Shirenewton, the Sheriff's New Town, is crystal clear.

Part of the fascination of old maps lies in the re-discovery of place-names no longer current. For instance, Saxton and many later mappers mark Quenock chapel in the angle between the roads from Caerleon to Ponthir and to Usk. There is a reference in a chantry certificate in the reign of Edward VI to: *a little chapel called Saint Gwynog with lands and tenements given towards the finding of a priest.* This was in the mid-16th century and the chapel may have been there from the 14th century. No vestige remains, though Chapel Field on Cassandra or St Andrew's Farm marks the site. According to Bradney's HISTORY OF MONMOUTHSHIRE the Chapel was dedicated to St Andrew. Alas, poor Quenock.

The fascination is inexhaustible. Perhaps one has not previously noticed on Nathaniel Coltman's map in Coxe's HISTORY near Llanhiddel (sic) a surprising Castell Italorum — a Welsh-Latin description of a Roman fort?

Mid-19th century maps still show two parts of Herefordshire within Monmouthshire: Crooked Billet and Bwlch Trewyn. The first lies astride the high road between Devauden and Trellech, a restricted area recalled nowadays only in the name of a local cottage. The second, north of Abergavenny, adjoins another enclave of Herefordshire in the former Breconshire called the Fothok, a corruption of the Welsh Fwddog.

In 1844, Crooked Billet and Bwlch Trewyn were legally transferred to Monmouthshire in exchange for Welsh Bicknor hitherto a Monmouthshire outpost in Herefordshire. Welsh Bicknor was Lann Custenhinn-garth-Benni (Constantine) of the 12th century BOOK OF LLANDAFF which quoted a dubious 6th century Charter of King Pebiau granting it to the See of Llandaff *for ever* and adding a Latin warning that God would destroy anyone who failed to observe the grant. The warning went unheeded by the tidy-minded 19th century legislators.

Place-names in Monmouthshire have always provided cartographers with problems. They merit our sympathy from Saxton on — whose warrant indicated that he was to have in Wales the services of a bi-lingual horseman. The man was to give the local name in Welsh; Saxton would then write down what he thought the name sounded like.

Hence down the centuries, the naming — and the mis-naming — of Monmouthshire.

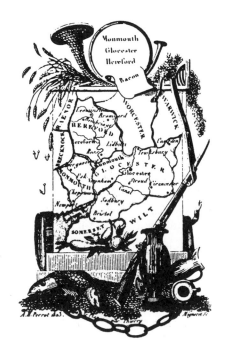

A.N. Perrot, 1823

The Maps of Monmouthshire

CHRISTOPHER SAXTON (? 1542 — ? 1620)   1577

Size: 15.1 x 18.7 inches (380 x 470 mm)   Scale of miles: 8 = 4.4 inches
                                                              1 mile = 0.55 inches

This is the earliest extant map of the County from Saxton's original survey engraved by one of a London-based team of engravers. The date 1577 on the map reinforces other evidence that many of Saxton's 34 county maps of England and Wales were already drawn and separately available for sale well before the appearance of the collected edition in 1579.

The title *MONUMETHENSIS COMITATUS REGIS HENRICI QUINTI NATALITIIS CELEBERRIMUS* Ano. Dni. 1577, alluding to the County's greatest fame as birth-place at Monmouth in 1387 of Henry V, is engraved top left in an architectural panel with a female and a male figure, perhaps Eve and Adam, to the left and the right standing on small globes. Clusters of fruit hang from either end of the entablature which they appear to support. The panel is surmounted by the royal arms of Queen Elizabeth I having a rampant lion and dragon.

Lower, to the left, are the arms of Thomas Seckford, Saxton's financial backer, beneath a scroll with the motto *Industria Naturam Ornat*, Industry improves Nature.

Bottom left, the *scala miliarum*, the scale of miles, is surmounted by a pair of dividers in front of a decorative band bearing the words *Christophorus Saxton descripsit*.

Two sailing ships to the right of the centre fold decorate the stippled Bristol Channel, here titled simply *Sabrina flu.*, the river Severn. There are two types of lettering: larger capitals for towns, script for other locations. Hills are conically represented in profile; parks are fenced; trees and towers and conventionally drawn houses represent woodland and buildings respectively. Bridges, but not roads, are marked. North, East, South and West are indicated in the ornamental borders by their latin names, *septentrio, oriens, meridies, occidens*.

There were several impressions of the first edition of the SAXTON ATLAS of 1579 and some county maps continued to be issued separately. The British Library, for example, has six impressions of the 1577 map of Monmouthshire by Saxton. It is difficult, and perhaps now impossible, to identify the different impressions of the first edition with any precision. It is suggested, but cannot be proved, that those copies of the map are earliest that have in the paper the bunch of grapes watermark; other watermarks, possibly later, include crossed arrows and a kneeling saint with a cross. The absence of a watermark need not rule out the authenticity of an early map since, in the very large sheets used, the watermark might lie outside the smaller area on which the map appears.

Special attention must be drawn to a lively scene on the Skirrid Mountain, near Abergavenny. This features four men and six animals, five of which appear to be hounds chasing the sixth, a fox.

Christopher Saxton fathered a family of maps which continually updated his original plates until they finally became too worn to be effective in the hands of Dicey and Company in 1770.

SAXTON / WEB   Another edition.   1642

MONUMETHENSIS COMITATUS REGIS HENRICI QUINTI NATALITIIS CELEBERRIMUS.
This is one of *The maps of all the Shires in England and Wales. Exactly taken and truly described by Christopher Saxton. And graven at the charges of a private gentleman for the publicke good. Now newly revised, amended and reprinted. Printed for William Web at the Globe in Cornhill, 1645.* The arms of Charles I replace those of Elizabeth I in this so-called Civil War atlas.

The date 1577 on Saxton's map has been altered to 1642.

Web's name does not appear on the map.

MONMOUTHSHIRE ..... by C.S. (Christopher Saxton). Corrected and amended by P. Lea.
This map is from THE SHIRES OF ENGLAND AND WALES *described by Christopher Saxton. Being the Best and Original Maps. With Many Additions and Corrections viz: ye Hund*(reds), *Road, etc. by Philip Lea...* (1690).
Lea adds C.R. (Carolus Rex) to Web's Royal Arms. He replaces the arms of Seckford with the Prince of Wales's feathered plume and the arms of R. Cary, Earl of Monmouth, and James Scott, Duke of Monmouth.
Apart from showing Hundreds and principal roads for the first time, Lea also introduces Speed's plan of Monmouth, stealing a good idea.
Lea presumably had access to the Saxton plate of Monmouthshire revised about 1665 for an edition of Saxton's atlas that was never published.
Lea published a second edition of his 1690 atlas in 1694.

SAXTON / WILLDEY   Another edition.   c.1720
George Willdey took over the remaining usable Saxton plates after the death of Philip Lea.
The title of the Atlas (1720) is almost identical with that of Lea.

C. DICEY   The last issue.   c.1770
Willdey's name has been erased.

REPRODUCTIONS
Facsimiles of the first edition, so marked bottom centre, were issued by the British Museum in 1935; also in 1959; also in 1964.

Playing Cards — A Note

Hand-painted packs of cards of high artistic quality were made from about 1450. The next stage was to use playing-cards for educational purposes. William Bowes seems to have been the first to see the useful connection between 52 cards and the Counties of England and Wales.

WILLIAM BOWES   1590; c.1605
Size of map: 1.2 x 1.2 inches
Maps based on Saxton maps of England and Wales. *MONMUTH* (sic) (Monmouthshire): Four of Hearts.   Compass and topographical notes added.

MORDEN   1676; 1680
Monmouth(shire): King of Spades.
Morden uses Saxton, with modifications by Speed, Blome, Ogilby.

REDMAYNE   1676; 1677; 1711-12
Monmouth(shire): Seven of Spades.

LENTHALL   1711?
Monmouth(shire): King of Spades.

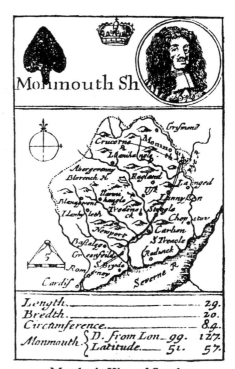

Morden's King of Spades

PIETER VAN DEN KEERE (c.1571 — 1646)   c.1605

Size: 3.3 x 4.7 inches (850 x 120 mm)   Scale of miles: 8 = 2 inches

MONMOUTHSHIRE (Monumenthensis Comitatus) was among the first collection of 44 County maps based on Saxton engraved by Van den Keere probably in Amsterdam in the first decade of the 17th century.   In 1617 Joan Blaeu used the same plates in his epitome of Camden's BRITANNIA published in Amsterdam.   Whereas the earlier impression had a blank verso, a Latin text now appears.

About 1619, George Humble secured the Dutch plates for the first English publication. The title of his atlas of 57 maps read: ENGLAND; WALES AND IRELAND: *their several counties abridged from a farr larger vollume by John Speed.*   The title was incorrect since it was largely the maps additional to the original 44 that were derived from Speed.   The maps had English titles and plate numbers: *Moumouthshire* (sic) was number 44. The backs were plain and there was no text.

In 1627, Humble produced three editions containing 63 maps, now following the order of Speed's THEATRE and borrowing the wording of his text.   Monmouthshire, now plate 48, has three paragraphs of the description of Glamorganshire printed in English on the reverse.

The original plates were beginning to show signs of wear, but there were further editions of Van den Keere in 1632, 1646, 1662 (when Roger Rea took over from Humble), c.1665, 1666, 1668, 1676 (the last issue by Thomas Bassett and Richard Chiswell).

Mr Robert Davies, of the National Library of Wales, identifies the separate editions of the Monmouthshire map, plate 48, by the varying width of the caption Glamorgan—shire in the re-set texts expressed in centimetres as follows: 1627, 7.0 cm; 1632, 7.5 cm; 1646, 1662 and 1665, 6.1 cm; 1666 and 1668, 5.1 cm; 1676, 4.5 cm.

WILLIAM CAMDEN (1551 — 1623) / WILLIAM HOLE   1607

Size: 12.7 x 13.3 inches (323 x 335 mm)   Scale: 8 miles = 3.28 inches

The title is: *MONUMETHENSIS COMITATUS QUEM OLIM INCOLUERUNT SILURES. Christophorus Saxton descripsit. Gulielmus Hole sculpsit.*   This title below the Royal arms top left describes the county as the former home of the Silurian tribe of pre-Roman Celts.

Although Camden, Headmaster of Westminster School, was said to have completed a set of county maps before the turn of the century, the sixth and last Latin edition of his BRITANNIA (first edition, 1586) was the first in which maps were included, engraved generally either by William Hole or by William Kip.

The engravers based their work on Saxton. Although they were working within reduced length and breadth, they succeeded in rendering the details remarkably clearly. In some instances the spelling, assiduously copied from Saxton, is more legible! But the hunting scene on the Skirrid Mountain is not included.

The Royal arms now incorporate, in place of the Welsh dragon, the Scottish unicorn, as an indication that James IV of Scotland was now James I of England.   Below the two beasts is the inscription: *Beat: pacifici, Blessed are the peacemakers.*

Dividers rest upon the scale of miles, bottom left. A noble vessel rides the Severn Channel, *Sabrinae Aestuarium.*   An ornamental compass-box appears bottom right.

The Camden/Hole map of 1607 has a Latin text printed on the back.

The English edition of 1610 has no printed text. Another state of the 1610 map and the edition of 1637 carry plate numbers. Monmouthshire is plate no.37. Mr Robert Davies, National Library of Wales, draws attention to the difference in the engraving of the estuaries: double lines in 1610; thick single lines in 1637.

35

Size: 14.4 x 19.4 inches (366 x 494 mm)   Scale: 5 miles = 2.8 inches

The county maps in Speed's magnificent THE THEATRE OF THE EMPIRE OF GREAT BRITAIN, engraved in Amsterdam chiefly by Jodocus Hondius, but printed with accompanying text in London, were not the result of a new survey. Speed admits, "I have put my sickle into other men's corn".

Speed relied on Saxton and earlier cartographers and writers. However, he included plans of towns — in Monmouthshire of Monmouth itself — boundaries and names of Hundreds. On the back of each map there is a precis of what Camden had to say about the County, a list of Hundreds, and an index of parishes, giving their locations within Hundreds.

Separate county maps were available before the complete collection appeared in the first edition about 1610.

The Countye of Monmouth ... Performed by John Speede ... sold by John Sudbury and George Humble is enhanced as a map not only by the town-plan of Monmouth in a cartouche top left, but also by a portrait of Henry V in a decorated roundel suspended from the cartouche, by the royal arms over the title top right and by seals, bottom left and right, containing separately the four lions *passant-gardant* of the Prince of Wales and the three feathers with the *Ich Dien* motto of the Black Prince.

Improbable female figures sit on either side of the Severn holding mathematical instruments. A ship under full sail graces the shaded wavy waters, this latter moiré device being typical of Dutch engravers, particularly Hondius. The four strap-work borders carry in central panels the cardinal points, but a small circular compass-indicator appears only in the inset Monmouth plan, together with a scale of *pases* (sic). Speed claims that the presence of a scale of paces on any of his maps may be taken to indicate that he both paced and drew the town plan himself. Incidentally, Speed's map of Wales, 1611, has illustrations of 16 Welsh towns, but not of Monmouth.

Editions and issues of his map carrying the names of Sudbury and Humble were available earlier, or not later than: 1610; 1616; c.1623; 1627; 1632 (with a slight reduction in the length of the printed title); 1646; 1650; 1651; 1652; 1653; 1654. The five impressions in the 1650's have one line between the two columns of text on the back.

The description of the County printed on the verso is in English up to and including the 1616 edition and in Latin thereafter. The 1616 edition has *Zuyth* for south on the bottom border.

Speed's maps found new vendors from 1650. The imprint now becomes: *Performed by John Speede and are to be sold by Roger Rea the Elder and younger at the Golden Cross in Cornhill against the Exchange*. The 1650 date is notional since again the new complete THEATRE seems not to have been issued until 1665. Separate maps anticipated the collection. The imprint panel on the map of Monmouthshire carries the date 1662!

In 1676, the THEATRE now bears the legend: *Performed by John Speed and are to be sold by Thomas Basset in Fleet Street and Richard Chiswell in Saint Paul's Church yard*. The arms of Robert Carey, Earl of Monmouth, and James Scot, Duke of Monmouth, are added.

In the intervening period, loose sheets without backing text were issued by Basset and Chiswell, perhaps by Christopher Browne, and certainly by John and Henry Overton, but the most important edition is by the last named, important for an innovation. Roads first appear on the edition of 1743, *sold by Henry Overton at the White Horse without Newgate London*.

Finally, apart from reproductions, C. Dicey made the last use of the now considerably re-touched Speed plates in 1770. *Sold by C. Dicey and Co: in Aldermary Church-Yard, London* appears on most of the 1770 County maps, but the imprint does not replace that of Overton on the map of Monmouthshire.

MICHAEL DRAYTON (1563 — 1631) / WILLIAM HOLE   c.1612

Size: 9.7 x 12.8 inches (247 x 326 mm)   No Scale.

There are three editions: 1612; 1613 (where this map has a page, not a plate, number 55) and 1622.

The map of Monmouthshire and Glamorganshire with part of Brecknockshire and a stretch of the West of England coast is one of eighteen illustrations to the same number of songs in Drayton's POLYOLBION (1612), versified topography. Since it has neither county boundaries, nor scale, nor compass indication, it is better described as a cartographical curiosity.

It features inaccurately named and placed rivers and four Monmouthshire mountains: *Tamberlow, Blorench, Penvaile* and *Skirriduaure* (sic). Rustics sit or stand on the heights; bare nymphs emerge from the streams. William Hole has engraved small waves convincingly to represent the sea.

Across the dividing Severn, where Neptune and one of his mistresses balance separately on monstrous sea-creatures; where a bird, presumably a puffin, perches on the head of Lundy's own nymph; and whence Sabrina emerges from her river, two vast crowds of instrumentalists and singers compete.

Drayton's introduction to his Fourth Song explains the cross-Channel confrontation:
England and Wales strive in this song
To whether (i.e. to which of the two) *Lundy doth belong.*
He continues:
The Britons chaunt King Arthur's glory
The English sing their Saxon's story.
The referee is Neptune. The Welsh team have strong support from hills and valleys, but the result is doubtful, unless a rather modern meaning is attached to the concluding word of the following couplet:
To keep the English part in awe
There's heave and shove and hold and draw.

JOHN BILL (1604 — 1630)   1626

Size: 3.4 x 4.6 inches (84 x 118 mm)   Scale: 8 miles = 0.95 inches

The map is in THE ABRIDGEMENT OF CAMDEN'S BRITANNIA WITH THE MAPS OF THE SEVERAL SHIRES OF ENGLAND AND WALES. *Printed by John Bill, printer to the King's most excellent majesty 1626.* There is no reprint.

The title is *MONMOUTH/SHIRE* and parts of adjoining counties are shown, but there is no indication of the name of Bill or any other. The map is based closely on Van den Keere, but is more crowded, partly because there was a better use of space in the earlier map, several place-names being set at an angle.

This is the earliest county map to show latitude and longitude. The former is indicated on the left border divided into sections of five minutes. The longitude is based on a prime meridian passing through the Azores — Greenwich was adopted later — and is marked off in degrees and minutes along the bottom border. A pair of dividers straddles the scale of miles; the cardinal points are named outside the four borders.

The plate has the description of Glamorganshire on its back. The text describing Monmouthshire is on the back of the Brecknockshire plate. We are told that the County has six Hundreds, one hundred and twenty seven parish churches, fifteen rivers, one chace, eight parks and six market towns.

Table of Distances and Road Maps — A Note

Until the second half of the 17th century, maps were intended to be looked at and enjoyed rather than carried and used. John Dee in 1570 in THE ENGLISH EUCLID speaks of maps, *to beautify Halls, Parkes, Chambers, Galeries, Studies or Libraries.* In 1621, Robert Burton writes, *Methinks it would well please any man to look upon a Geographicall map ... to behold as it were all the remote Provinces, Townes, Cities of the World.*

But Robert Herrick in a poem to his brother Nicholas, written about 1648, contrasts his own stay-at-home acquaintance with mere *varnished maps* and his travelled brother's direct familiarity with the places depicted. The utility rather than the appearance of maps was becoming paramount. The outbreak of Civil War in 1642 had already increased the demand for regional maps of Britain, nor were these of much value unless roads and distances were indicated.

In 1635 Matthew Simmons, and in 1643 Thomas Jenner, issued tiny local maps with triangular distance tables engraved by Van Langeren. Neither in the first nor subsequent editions of Simmons, or of Jenner, is there a map of Monmouthshire.

However, an important step forward was taken by John Ogilby (1600—1675). He completed a few county maps, but Monmouthshire was not among them. In 1675 Ogilby published his BRITANNIA, VOLUME THE FIRST. Plate 16 showed in a series of parallel, vertical scrolls the road from Monmouth via Newport and Cardiff to Burton Ferry (Briton Ferry). It travels over Wentwood dropping into Newport from Christchurch Hill. Alongside Ogilby's strip-roads places of interest are richly indicated.

Speed and Saxton are abandoned. Ogilby's surveyors pushed *wheel dimensurators* along roads to give reasonably accurate distances. What is more, the Statute Mile of 1,760 yards authorised by the Act of 1593 is now the standard. It is not our purpose to include later road maps, but Ogilby cannot be overlooked. His work was beneficial to all later county map cartographers, as several of them acknowledged in print. Thomas Gardner and others published reduced versions.

Ogilby was also among the first who contested continental supremacy in the field of map-making. Sheet-maps and bound atlases were originally imported by London booksellers from Antwerp, Amsterdam and elsewhere. Later London booksellers began to employ their own surveyors, artists and engravers, foreign and native. If they paid for the map-plates, book-sellers became owners, sometimes fortified by royal patents and privileges, and could themselves become publishers and, if they had presses, printers also. As many maps indicate, a variety of trades was more commonly involved.

Competing tradesmen multiplied from the Commonweath on. But the influence of Saxton and Speed did not die quickly. Pepys was ahead of his time; his maps were behind it. When he faced the problem of carriage of timber from the Forest of Dean, as his DIARY for June 20th 1662 indicates, he turned to his copy of Speed.

Decorative Scale of Miles

Size: 14.6 x 19.4 inches (372 x 493 mm)   Scale: 4 English miles (1 German mile) = 2.2 inches

MONUMETHENSIS COMITATUS. VERNACULE MONMOUTH SHIRE.   Based on Speed (post 1623), but *Sabrinae Aestuarium* now replaced by *Sabrinae Ostium*. Signed *I Blaeu exc.* bottom right.

Latin atlas of 1645 entitled: GUIL. ET IOANNIS/BLAEU/THEATRUM/ORBIS TERRARUM/ SIVE ATLAS NOVUS/PARS QUARTA/AMSTERDAMI. APUD IOHANN BLAEU. Dated 1645 in Roman numerals. Variations in titles of later atlases in other languages.

The Latin text of Camden's BRITANNIA is on the back of the 1645 map, but is lacking in some later bound atlases and on some loose sheets. The text is found in a variety of languages: in Latin, 1645, 1646, 1648, 1662; in French, 1645, 1646, 1648, 1662, 1663, 1667; in German, 1646, 1648; in Dutch, 1647, 1648; in Spanish, 1659, 1662. Variations in the pagination and in the letter press help to date Blaeu's maps more precisely. One other rough guide is that in mid-century the long S gives place to the short S.

Blaeu follows Speed in showing Hundreds, but not roads. The sea is, however, unshaded. The symbols for hills and trees are smaller than Speed's, but more numerous. Blaeu omits the town plan of Monmouth, but includes the royal arms top left and, top right, the three Prince of Wales feathers below the arms of Wales. Something seems to have gone wrong in the colour coding for the latter. Where Speed had the lions quartered correctly and, where coloured, two red on gold (*gules on or*) and two gold on red, Blaeu's earliest colourists mistakenly have golden lions on a red shield.

Blacu's map has decorative country scenes bottom left and bottom right, not especially connected with Monmouthshire. Everywhere the calligraphic quality is superb and artistic balance pleasing.

A disastrous fire in 1672 is believed to have destroyed not only the premises of the Blaeu family but also the copper printing plates on which the county maps were engraved.

Size: 15.8 x 20 inches (402 x 508 mm)   Scale: 10 miles = 3.1 inches
                                                           (English miles — 4 constitute one German mile)
GLOCESTRIA DUCATUS, CUM MONUMETHENSI COMITATU. GLOCESTER SHIRE (sic) *AND MONMOUTH SHIRE.*

IOANNIS IANSSONII NOVUS ATLAS, SIVE THEATRUM ORBIS TERRARUM: IN QUO MAGNA BRITANNIA, SEU ANGLIAE ET SCOTIAE NEC NON HIBERNIAE, REGNA EXHIBENTUR. Latin edition, Amsterdam, 1646 and 1659.

French editions 1646, 1647, 1652 and 1656; German, 1647, 1652 (actually issued 1658); Dutch, 1647, 1649, 1652, 1653, 1659.

Gerard Valck and Pieter Schenk issued and sold separately loose sheets after 1681, without Camden's description of the county which appeared in the appropriate language in atlases listed above. Atlases in French were also issued in 1714 and 1715 (David Mortier) and in 1724 (Joseph Smith). Page numbers vary slightly in different editions and may assist identification.

Country scenes surround the scroll bearing the scale of miles top left. Bottom right, a goddess and three cherubs surround the royal arms over the title of the map. A distinctive feature is the row of ten shields across the top bearing the arms of eight earls and two dukes of Gloucester. One blank shield is suspended below these, perhaps for the purchaser to fill in his own arms.

There was intense rivalry between the houses of Blaeu and of Jansson; this competition raised the artistic standards of both. Jansson did not hesitate to copy from Blaeu; both copied from Speed.

The Dutch engravers must have found the copying of names in an obscure language tiresome and mistakes were made. For example Coedkernew, South-west of Newport, is spelt *Coydkirne* by Saxton, Speed and Blaeu. Jansson has *Coydkinne*.

RICHARD BLOME (1641 — 1705)

Size: 12.2 x 9.5 inches (310 x 242 mm)   Scale: 4 miles = 1.8 inches

A MAP OF YE COUNTY OF MONMOUTH SHIRE WITH HUNDREDS BY RIC. BLOME BY HIS MAJESTY'S COMAND (sic).

From BRITANNIA: OR A GEOGRAPHICAL DESCRIPTION OF THE KINGDOMS OF ENGLAND, SCOTLAND AND IRELAND ... Illustrated with a map of each county of England, besides several general ones ... London, Richard Blome, 1673.

A further edition, London, John Wright, 1677.

Blome includes Monmouthshire as an English County; no Welsh county is included but there are general maps of North Wales and of South Wales. He exploited cartography without adding to its charm or accuracy. He wrongly forecast that Camden's BRITANNIA was unlikely to be printed; he described Speed as good, but out-moded, and proceeded to have it closely copied.

There are two ships under sail in the Severn Sea which is unshaded. A garland surrounds the arms of William Morgan of Tredegar and Machen etc. to whom Blome dedicates his map. Blome shrewdly dedicates a later imprint to Edward Proger Esquire, one of Charles II's cronies, who died aged 96 early in 1714.

RICHARD BLOME

Size: 9.3 x 7.3 inches (237 x 186 mm)   4 miles = 1.3 inches

A MAP OF YE COUNTY OF MONMOUTH WITH ITS HUNDREDS. FROM SPEED'S MAPS EPITOMIZED OR THE MAPS OF THE COUNTIES OF ENGLAND. *ALPHABETICALLY PLACED. LONDON. PRINTED ANN. DOM. 1681.*

Blome's name does not appear on the map which is even more crudely drawn than the earlier and larger map. If it is after Speed, it is a long way after. A compass indicator has been added, lower left. The first edition of 1681 was dedicated to James Duke of Monmouth.

There were later editions of the smaller Blome in 1685 (London, Samuel Lownes); 1693 (London, Richard Blome); 1715 (London, Thomas Taylor — when the plate number 25 appears in the top right corner); 1716 (when Taylor adds roads for the first time). The smaller Blome was more successful than the larger and was again published in 1750 by Thomas Bakewell.

JOHN SELLER (? 1658 — 1698)

Size: 4.7 x 5.7 inches (120 x 145 mm)   Scale: 5 miles = 0.75 inches

MONMOUTHSHIRE by John Seller.

From ANGLIA CONTRACTA, or *A Description of the Kingdom of England and Principality of Wales in Several New Mapps of All the Countyes therein contained by John Seller (1694).*

Reprinted 1696 (John Gwillim); 1697 (H. Newman); 1701 (Joseph Wild); 1703 (J. Marshall). Seller/Grose 1777 embodies Seller's map with a text below and continued on the back. The map is divided into 5 mile squares. There is a compass indicator in the Severn. Parts of all the adjoining counties appear and many Glamorgan locations are included from Cardiff up to *Martertiduel* (Merthyr Tydfil). Seller is not as generous with Monmouthshire names on the corresponding Glamorganshire map.

Six Hundreds are listed lower left: A, *Abergavenny;* B, *Skenfrith;* C, *Ragland;* D, *Caldicott;* E, *Wentlooge;* F, *Uske.*

Seller was the Royal Hydrographer responsible for the issue of many charts and maps. Some original surveying seems to have been undertaken under his guidance. Seller based his maps on the meridian of London (St. Paul's) in place of the Azores, though this improvement is not indicated on his Monmouthshire map.

ROBERT MORDEN (? 1650 — 1703)   1695

Size: 13.6 x 16.2 inches (346 x 412 mm)   Scale: 5 miles = Small 2.1", Middle 2.4", Great 2.7"

THE COUNTY OF MONMOUTH By Robt. Morden. Sold by Abel Swale Awnsham and John Churchil.

In Camden's BRITANNIA, 1695, by Edmund Gibson. Facsimile, David and Charles, 1971. Newly translated in 1695 from the Latin BRITANNIA of 1586. The prospectus promised that the Morden maps would *alone be worth the money*, but many of the maps were available in loose sheets prior to publication in 1695 — there was no backing text.

The claim that this County map is from a new survey seems hardly justified. The first drafts of the Morden maps are reputed to have been sent to regional experts *with a request to supply the defects, rectify the positions, and correct the false spellings.* Morden had little help from Monmouthshire men or disregarded advice. The spelling, for example, is as erratic as ever, though it may have been the engraver who perpetrated *Heullis* for Henllys (corrected later) and who turned Gelligaer just over the border into *Rethlygaier!*

The debt to the Elizabethans — particularly to Speed — and to the Jacobeans remains heavy. But longitude is now measured along the bottom border from the meridian of London (St. Paul's). The difference in local time is also indicated along the top border. A few roads are imprecisely indicated by single lines. Note the optional mileages!

After 1695, there were editions of the "Larger" Morden in 1722, ? 1730, 1753 and 1772. There was continuous re-touching of the plates and some revision of place-names.

ROBERT MORDEN   1701

Size: 6.2 x 8.1 inches (156 x 205 mm)   Scale: 6 miles = 1.5 inches

MONMOUTH SHIRE by Robt. Morden. Plate no. 25.

THE NEW DESCRIPTION AND STATE OF ENGLAND, *containing the mapps of the Counties of England and Wales, in Fifty Three Copper Plates, Newly Designed, Exactly Drawn and Engraven by the Best Artists ...*, Robert Morden, Thomas Cockerill and Ralph Smith 1701.

Later editions, 1704, 1708 (Hermann Moll), 1720, 1730, 1738. The "Smaller" Morden continued to be incorporated in other topographical works during the 18th century.

It seems probable that the maps were intended for the 1695 BRITANNIA, but were rejected as being too small. Certainly the Monmouthshire map is very crowded, even though a supplementary list of twenty-one places, indicated only by letters of the alphabet on the map, is given bottom left. And capital *C, Ch* and *Chu* are said to stand for Castle, Chapel and Church respectively.

A compass indicator and more roads are added from 1708 onwards, when the maps are described as, *Begun by Mr Morden: perfected, corrected and enlarged by Mr Moll.* The words *To Llanbedr* from Abergavenny, and *To St Davids* from Newport, are printed upside down. A dotted line indicates the Aust Ferry linking Monmouthshire, via Chepstow, with Bristol.

EMANUEL BOWEN *Floruit* 1720 — 1767   1720

Size: 3.5 x 4.3 inches (89 x 109 mm)   Scale: 6 miles = 0.8 inches

Within an ornamental panel above the map proper, there is a table of distances on the road from Monmouth to *Llanbedr* (Lampeter), *containing 48 miles computed and 68 miles 4 furlongs measured!* From Monmouth the road proceeds west through Llantilio Crossenny and Abergavenny. *Redbrue* is evidently Sennybridge; remaining places are easily identified.

The map and road details are from BRITANNIA DEPICTA OR OGILBY IMPROVED. 1720, plate no. 20.

Apart from Ogilby (1625), which was not easily portable, there had been other early 18th century attempts to produce smaller road-books. Two worth noting are those of John Senex in his ACTUAL SURVEY OF ALL PRINCIPAL ROADS OF ENGLAND AND WALES (1719) and of Thomas Gardner in a POCKET GUIDE TO THE ENGLISH TRAVELLER (also 1719).

Emanuel Bowen was one of the most skilled and artistic of 18th century cartographers. He was also a print-seller and, with the co-operation of his publisher, John Owen, who probably wrote the descriptive material, he produced a pocketable volume by having his miniature maps printed on both sides of the page together with road lengths and a brief account of the County portrayed. There is a seven-line description of Monmouthshire:

The Air is healthful and temperate; the soil is hilly and woody; the valleys fruitful...

His place-names are necessarily crowded, but clearly engraved. Main roads and rivers stand out clearly enough for rider or walker.

Chubb lists reprints and editions of "Owen and Bowen" in 1720, 1721 (second edition), 1723 (third edition), 1724 (fourth edition), 1730, 1731, 1734, 1736, 1749, 1751, 1753, 1759, 1764 (fifth edition).

There are also "Owen and Bowen" maps giving chiefly the road details. Plate no. 37 in the series bears the Arms of the Bishop of Llandaff and, following Ogilby, depicts the road from Monmouth via Christchurch, Newport, and then via Bassaleg to Cardiff.

HERMAN MOLL *Floruit*, 1688 — 1732   1724

Size: 7.5 x 10 inches (191 x 254 mm)   Scale: 10 miles = 2.3 inches

MONMOUTH/SHIRE by H. Moll, Geographer, in a rectangle top left. Below this, a list of six Hundreds, lettered A to F: *Bergavenni, Skenfrith, Wentloge, Uske, Caldecott.* Scale of miles, bottom right. Lines of latitude and longitude.

Outside the map, left and right, are six archaeological drawings, all save one from *Kaer Lheion* (Caerleon): A Phiala or Bowl; a Chequer'd (i.e. mosaic) Pavement; the Alabaster Statue found near Porch Shini (sic); Roman Fibula; Another View of the Same (Fibula); Fragment of an Altar. Camden describes and illustrates the damaged alabaster statue, found across the Usk from Caerleon below Christchurch *near a place called Porth Sini Krân.* He says that originally the figure appears to have carried a sword and scales.

The Moll map is from A NEW DESCRIPTION OF ENGLAND AND WALES, *with the adjacent islands ... London. H. Moll, T. Bowles, C. Rivington and J. Bowles, 1724.*

Moll, a Dutchman, was himself the engraver. His spelling, particularly of words of Welsh derivation is understandably bizarre. The words *To Crickhowel* are inverted on one of the growing number of roads now drawn.

The fifty County maps were issued coloured in 1724. They were re-printed in the same year with the additional of a plate number (Monmouthshire being no. 38) but without colour.

There were later editions in 1733 and 1739; and in 1747 and 1753, minus the archaeological engravings. The first set of maps was contemporary with Daniel Defoe's TOUR THROUGH THE WHOLE ISLAND OF GREAT BRITAIN (1724—26).

THOMAS BADESLADE *Floruit* 1719 — 1745   1742

Size: 6.0 x 5.7 inches (152 x 132 mm)   Scale: 10 miles = 1.2 inches

The County map measures only 4.1 inches across, but there is to the left a panel of information about parliamentary representation and about markets and fairs in Monmouth, Abergavenny, Chepstow, Kaer Lheion (sic), Newport, Pontypool and Uske. Place-names are not profuse. There is a compass at the top.

The map reads, below its bottom border,: *T. Badeslade delin (eavit). Publish'd by the Proprietor W.H. Toms, Sept 29, 1742. W.H. Toms sculp*(sit). Its atlas is CHOROGRAPHIA BRITANNIAE OR A SET OF ALL THE COUNTIES IN ENGLAND AND WALES ... Thomas Badeslade surveyed and drew the map; William Henry Toms engraved it.

There appear to have been two editions of the 1742 map; the first edition proper bore the date 1741, but was reported to have been published in 1742. There were a further edition and new imprints in 1743, 1745 and 1749.

JOHN COWLEY *Floruit* 1734 — 1744   1744

Size: 6 x 5.4 inches (152 x 136 mm)   Scale: 6 miles = 1.1 inches

AN IMPROVED MAP OF MONMOUTH SHIRE containing the Borough and Market Towns with those Adjoyning; also its Principal Roads and Rivers, by I. Cowley Geogr. to his Majesty.
Compass top left. Explanation (symbols for Boroughs, Market Towns, Castles) and Scale of Miles bottom right. Borders with latitudes and longitudes.
The spelling of place-names is carelessly inaccurate e.g. *Brewefield Cast.* for Greenfield (Maesglas) Castle; *Trintern* for Tintern (Moll has *Trintirn*); *Matheon* for Mathern.
THE GEOGRAPHY OF ENGLAND: *done in the manner of Gorton's geographical grammar ... To each county is prefix'd a compleat mapp from the latest and best observations, shewing the chief towns, parks, rivers and roads, both direct and across. London. R. Dodsley, 1744.*
Also to be found in A NEW SETT OF POCKET MAPPS OF ALL THE COUNTIES OF ENGLAND AND WALES, *London. R. Dodsley and M. Cooper, 1745.*

JOHN ROCQUE *Floruit* 1734 — 1762   1746

Size: 5.9 x 7.4 inches (150 x 188 mm)   Scale: 10 miles = 1.8 inches

MONMOUTH SHIRE top centre, outside the border. Scale of miles bottom right. Compass top left. Some roads shown. Hundreds not indicated. The hills are hatched in such a way as to indicate steepness by the closeness of the engraved lines.
Neither publisher's nor engraver's name appears.
Rocque, a Frenchman, was surveyor, engraver and publisher. From about 1734, he lived in London and in Dublin and was appointed Cartographer to the Prince of Wales, later George III.
THE ENGLISH TRAVELLER: *giving a description of those parts of Great-Britain called England and Wales. Containing ... a map of every county, from the best and latest observations ... after the designs of Herman Moll. London, T(homas) Read, 1746.*
A later edition, also in 1746, adds the plate-number 49 which later still in THE SMALL BRITISH ATLAS, 1753, London, John Rocque and Robert Sayer, is half erased, but in the 1762 and 1764 editions of that work is restored.   Finally, the plate number is again erased in ENGLAND DISPLAYED ... *By a society of gentlemen ... revised, corrected and improved by P. Russell, Esq., and Mr. Owen Price.*

ROBERT WALKER   1746

Size: 6 x 7.7 inches (152 x 195 mm)   Scale: 10 miles = 1.10 inches

Top left, the Arms of the town of Monmouth. Bottom left a compass. Scale of miles bottom right. Walker/Simpson is very similar to Read/Rocque and is also based on Moll. For example, *To Crickhowel* is similarly printed upside down, but the Moor becomes *the More*. *Wensewood* is mis-spelt.
There is no name of engraver or publisher on the map.
THE AGREEABLE HISTORIAN, OR THE COMPLEAT ENGLISH TRAVELLER: *giving a geographical description of every county in that part of Great Britain, called England ... with a map of every county prefixed to each, from the best and latest observations, after the designs of Herman Moll and others ... By Samuel Simpson, gent. London, printed by R. Walker, 1746.* Monmouthshire's is the last map in the third of the three volumes.

Size: 5.6 x 6.6 inches (142 x 165 mm)   Scale: 10 miles = 1.6 inches

A CORRECT MAP OF MONMOUTHSHIRE in engraved rectangular frame, top left. Compass indicator and scale of miles, bottom left. Plate number 24 outside margin, top right corner. The hills are shown as in Saxton. The quality of the engraving is good; place-names, rivers and roads stand out clearly.

There is no name of engraver or publisher on the map. *T. Hutchinson sculp.* appears in this series on the maps of Gloucestershire and of England and Wales. Stylistically, it seems certain that Hutchinson engraved this map.

GEOGRAPHIA MAGNAE BRITANNIAE. *Or, correct maps of all the counties in England, Scotland and Wales ... London, 1748.*   Thomas Osborne and six other co-publishers are named.

There is a second edition of the atlas also dated 1748, but not issued until 1756. Osborne now has seven associated publishers.

THOMAS KITCHIN   *Floruit* 1738 — 1776   1748

Size: 8.5 x 6.3 inches (216 x 160 mm)   Scale: 8 miles = 1.8 inches

MONMOUTH SHIRE. *Drawn from the Best Authorities, By T. Kitchin Geographer.*
Arms of Monmouth. Scale of miles, compass, Key, bottom right. Plate no. 33.
THE LONDON MAGAZINE: *or Gentleman's Monthly Intelligencer.   London, R. Baldwin* (1747—60).
Second edition HISTORICAL DESCRIPTIONS OF NEW AND ELEGANT PICTURESQUE VIEWS OF THE ANTIQUITIES OF ENGLAND AND WALES ... *published under the inspection of Henry Boswell, Esq., (and others). London, Alexander Hogg* (1786).
Later editions, with slightly varied atlas titles: 1790 and 1795 London, Alexander Hogg; 1798, Francis Grose replaces Henry Boswell and the name of H.D. Symonds is added to that of Hogg.

THOMAS JEFFERYS (*Floruit* 1732 — 1771) and THOMAS KITCHIN   1749

Size: 5.1 x 5.2 inches (130 x 132 mm)   Scale: 10 miles = 0.9 inches

Below the map are engraved particulars of fairs and markets in Monmouth and in six other places (Chepstow, Abergavenny, Pontypool, Kaer Lheion (sic), Newport, Uske). It is explained that there are two Members of Parliament for the County and one for the Borough of Monmouth. Compass top left. Scale of miles, bottom right. Hundreds not marked.

No name of engraver or publisher appears on the map. Jefferys himself seems at various times to have been surveyor, engraver and publisher.

THE SMALL ENGLISH ATLAS in which this map was intended to appear was issued in twelve parts weekly from November 1748. There were further editions in 1749 and 1751 (when a plate number 24 was added outside the border top right).

In 1775, THE SMALL ENGLISH ATLAS was taken over by Robert Sayer and John Bennett, John Bowes and Carington Bowles. In the later editions of 1785 and 1787 only the name of Robert Sayer appeared in the Atlas, of which there was a re-issue by Laurie and Whittle as late as 1794.

Jefferys used the Greenwich meridian in place of that of St. Paul's, adopted by Seller. Jefferys has described elsewhere how he used theodolite, chain and "plain table".

Size: 26.3 x 20.4 inches (665 x 518 mm)

Scale: 10 miles = 3.6 inches
69½ British Statute miles to a Degree.
(Measurement first used by Senex in 1721 in place
of earlier 60 miles to a degree)

AN ACCURATE MAP OF THE COUNTIES OF GLOUCESTER AND MONMOUTH.
Description of the Counties top left. Rural scene bottom right.

Dedicated to the Honourable John Thynne How, Lord Chedworth, with his Arms. Historical and topographical notes (see below).

Printed for John Bowles in Cornhill, Carington Bowles in St. Paul's Church Yard, Robert Sayer at the Golden Buck in Fleet Street.

THE LARGE ENGLISH ATLAS: OR A NEW SET OF MAPS OF ALL THE COUNTIES OF ENGLAND AND WALES ... *Each Map is Illustrated with a General Description of the County, its Cities, Borough and Market Towns, the Number of Members returned to Parliament, of Parishes, Houses, Acres of Lands, etc...*

Other editions: 1755, 1760, 1762, 1763, 1764, 1765, 1780, 1787, 1794.

EMANUEL BOWEN *Floruit* 1720 — 1767 1752

Size: 7 x 7.8 inches (178 x 198 mm)

Scale: 9 miles = 1.5 inches

MONMOUTHSHIRE. Drawn from the Best Authorities by Eman. Bowen, Geogr. to His Majesty (George II). Title in ornamental scroll, top left. The Arms of Monmouth, top right. Compass, centre right. Explanation of symbols used, lower right.

Outside the bottom border, *Printed for I. Hinton at the King's Arms in Newgate Street, 1752.* Above the top border, *Engraved for the Universal Magazine.*

The place-names are over-crowded. Despite the *Explanation*, there is insufficient difference between Great and Direct Post Roads and Principal Cross Roads.

THE UNIVERSAL MAGAZINE OF KNOWLEDGE AND PLEASURE ... *Published Monthly according to Act of Parliament, For John Hinton, at the King's Arms in St. Paul's Church Yard, London.* The map of Monmouthshire, though not numbered, was no. 24 in the set of 51, several of which were engraved by Thomas Kitchin and some by R.W. Seale.

GEORGE BICKHAM 1753

Size: 8.6 x 5.9 inches (218 x 150 mm)

No scale of Miles

A MAP OF MONMOUTHSHIRE, West from London. Humbly Inscrib'd to the Honble. T. Morgan, Lord Lieutenant of ye. County.

Distance from London to Monmouth 127 miles, distances to a few other towns in the County. A list of the Seven Hundreds: *Bergrave* (Bergavenny), *Ragland, Wentlooge, Caldicott, Skenfrith, Uske and Nye* (? Trelech, represented as Nigh or Wye).

This is not a map but a panoramic view of the County from across the Severn, where only Thornbury is named. A statue, classical columns partly in ruins and exotic foliage decorate the foreground. On a separate page, there is a description of the County under the Arms of Monmouth with two gentlemen in period dress on either side.

First edition of THE BRITISH MONARCHY with the topographical engravings, 1754. The book previously published without the views in 1743 and 1748.

Second edition: A CURIOUS COLLECTION OF BIRDS-EYE VIEWS OF THE SEVERAL COUNTIES IN ENGLAND AND WALES ... *finely engraved on forty-six plates. By George Bickham, junior. London, Robert Laurie and James Whittle, 1796.* Information regarding the County above and below the view is deleted.

Size: 4.4 x 2.5 inches (112 x 63 mm) Scale: 10 miles = 0.7 inches

MONMOUTH SHIRE in ornamental scroll top left. Scale of miles, top right. Description of County below compass at bottom of map. Plate no. 24 above border, top right.

Description: *Monmouthshire is in the Diocese of Llandaff and is 24 miles long and 20 broad. It contains 6,490 Houses, 38,840 inhabitants, 127 Parishes, 7 Market Towns and sends 3 Members of Parliament. The Air is Healthy and Temperate, and the soil is fruitful especially in the Vallies* (sic).

NEW AND ACCURATE MAPS OF THE COUNTIES OF ENGLAND AND WALES *drawn from the latest surveys by J. Gibson. London, J. Newbery 1759.*

A later edition, *London, T. Carnan, 1770.*

EMANUEL BOWEN 1762

Size: 7.3 x 6.5 inches (185 x 165 mm) Scale: 8 miles = 1.4 inches

MONMOUTHSHIRE DIVIDED INTO HUNDREDS Containing the Market Towns, Rivers, Roads, etc. By Eman: Bowen, Geogr. to His Late Majesty (George II died 1760).

Title in ornamented panel, top left. Scale, top right. List of Seven Hundreds, left centre. Explanation (symbols for Towns and Post Stages), bottom left.

Below the bottom border, *Engraved for the General Magazine of Arts and Sciences for W. Owen at Temple Bar 1762.*

THE NATURAL HISTORY OF ENGLAND; *or A Description of each particular County In regard to the curious Productions of Nature and Art. Illustrated by a Map of each County ... By Benjamin Martin. London. W. Owen and the Author. 1763.*

The forty maps in this volume are variously dated 1756 to 1762. The Map of Monmouthshire is no. 40. Plates 38 and 39 are of South Wales and of North Wales. No other Welsh County appears.

PIETER MEIJER 1769

Size: 7.3 x 6.4 inches (185 x 165 mm) Scale: 8 English miles = 1.4 inches
  2 Dutch miles = 1.5 inches

This Dutch map is a close copy of the foregoing Emanuel Bowen map, 1762.

There is a Dutch inscription in an ornamental panel top left: *Het Graafschap Monmouthshire ...* Below bottom border, left, *L. Schenk, Jansz. Sculp. 1769.*

THOMAS KITCHIN 1763

Size: 9.8 x 7.1 inches (249 x 180 mm) Scale: 8 miles = 2.1 inches

A NEW MAP OF MONMOUTH SHIRE, Drawn from the best Authorities: By Tho. Kitchin Geogr. Engraver to H.R.H. the Duke of York.

Title in ornamental scroll, top right. Remarks, top left. Scale, top centre. Compass at bottom, centre.

Attractive map with well-defined roads and rivers. Light appears to fall on the hills from the west, leaving their eastern slopes in deep shadow, and giving the illusion of altitude. Place-names are spelt with growing accuracy.

ENGLAND ILLUSTRATED, OR, A COMPENDIUM OF THE NATURAL HISTORY, GEOGRAPHY, TOPOGRAPHY AND ANTIQUITIES ECCLESIASTICAL AND CIVIL, OF ENGLAND AND WALES. *With maps of the several counties ... London, R. and J. Dodsley, dated 1764 (but thought to have been published in December 1763).*

Kitchin's name is spelt Kitchen in the second edition of the atlas in 1765, now titled KITCHEN'S ENGLISH ATLAS ...

Note also KITCHIN'S POCKET ATLAS, 1769, the basis for Carington Bowles, 1785 (see next item).

EMANUEL BOWEN   c.1763

Size: 19.5 x 16 inches (495 x 406 mm)   Scale: 12 miles = 6.2 inches
                                                                    British Statute miles, 69 to a degree

In a rural setting, engraved top right: *AN ACCURATE MAP OF THE COUNTY OF MONMOUTH. Divided into Hundreds ... By E. Bowen, Geographer to his late Majesty* (George II).

Outside border bottom centre: *Printed for R. Sayer and J. Ryall ... T. Bowles ... J. Bowles and Son ... Mess. Bakewell and Parker ... H. Overton ... and T. Kitchin.*

Based on Thomas Kitchin. THE LARGE ENGLISH ATLAS, 1749. View of Llandaff Cathedral, top left; Key, compass, array of historical and topographical notes filling un-mapped spaces. Some detail, north of Bristol.

THE ROYAL ENGLISH ATLAS, *being a New and Accurate Set of Maps of all the Counties of South Britain. Drawn from Surveys ... Particularly Distinguishing more Fully and Accurately the Church Livings, than any other Maps hitherto Published ... (London. 1763).*

Second edition, 1777, reads below bottom border: *London. Printed for Robt. Sayer and John Bennett No. 53 Fleet Street John Bowles and Carington Bowles ... as the Act directs, 1st of June 1777.*

Later editions and imprints of THE ROYAL ATLAS: 1778, 1779, 1780, 1781, 1828. Publishers' names vary. Many of the above maps were sold as loose sheets.

JOSEPH ELLIS   1765

Size: 9.8 x 7.5 inches (249 x 190 mm)   Scale: 8 miles = 2.1 inches

A MODERN MAP OF MONMOUTHSHIRE. Drawn from the latest Surveys; Corrected and Improved by the best Authorities. Plate no. 30.

Title appears in a scroll resembling that of Thomas Kitchin's map of 1763, of which the whole is a close copy, but with the further backing of a rural scene. Remarks, scale, title and compass are placed in virtually the same positions as on Kitchin, 1763. Ellis's hills are more heavily delineated and he is more lavish with trees indicating woodlands.

Below the map, there is inscribed: *Printed for Carington Bowles in St. Paul's Church yard and Robt. Sayer in Fleet Street.* Joseph Ellis is the engraver, not named on the map.

THE NEW ENGLISH ATLAS, *being the completest sett of modern maps of England and Wales ... ever yet published; accurately drawn from actual surveys ... and engrav'd in the best manner by J. Ellis, and others, on fifty-four copper plates.* London, Robert Sayer and Carington Bowles, 1765.

Subsequently, under the title ELLIS'S ENGLISH ATLAS, there were further editions in 1766, 1768, 1773, 1777, 1785, 1786 and 1796.

EMANUEL BOWEN   1767

Size: 12.5 x 8.6 inches (310 x 219 mm)   Scale: 10 miles = 2.6 inches

MONMOUTH SHIRE, DIVIDED INTO HUNDREDS; Exhibiting the County Borough and Market Towns; Describing the Church Livings, with Concise Historical Extracts, relative to Trade, Manufacturers, etc., and other Improvements not inserted in any Half Sheet County Map Extant. By Eman. Bowen, Geographer to His Late Majesty, and Thos. Bowen. Engraved top right, No. 14.

Title in scroll, top left. Scale of miles, bottom left. Compass in Bristol Channel. Explanation towards top right, includes symbols for Rectories, Vicarages and Curacies; also Post Stages; Measured Distances between Principal Towns are said to be indicated, but are infrequent. All spaces in adjoining counties and the Channel are filled with information about the County of Monmouth, Monmouth, Aber Gavenny (sic) and Chepstow. Variety of styles of lettering in the copper plate.

ATLAS ANGLICANUS ... *by the late Emanuel Bowen ... and Thomas Bowen. London T. Kitchin. 1767.*

Second edition, 1770, adds outside bottom border: *Printed for T. Kitchin at no. 59 Holborn Hill, London.*

Third edition, 1785, Bowles's NEW MEDIUM ENGLISH ATLAS.

Fourth edition, c. 1793, Bowles and Carver.

Size: 7.8 x 6.2 inches (198 x 158 mm)   Scale: 10 miles = 2 inches

A NEW MAP OF MONMOUTH SHIRE Drawn from the Latest Authorities.   Below the bottom margin of this map, paired to the right with a map of Herefordshire, appears: *Published by Alexr. Hogg at the Kings Arms, no. 16 Paternoster Row.*   Above the maps is inscribed: *Engraved for* WALPOOLE'S NEW AND COMPLETE BRITISH TRAVELLER.   Conder is not named on the Monmouthshire map, but his name appears on the other maps in THE BRITISH TRAVELLER and it is safe to assume that he was the engraver of all the copper plates.

Mistakenly, the Arms, in the top left corner above the Remarks, are those of Montgomery.   The title above is in a rural setting.   The compass is engraved within the lower Bristol Channel.

THE NEW BRITISH TRAVELLER; OR, A COMPLETE MODERN UNIVERSAL DISPLAY OF GREAT BRITAIN AND IRELAND ... *The whole published under the immediate inspection of George Augustus Walpoole, Esq, assisted ... by David Wynne Evans, F.R.S. ... Alexander Burnet, L.L.D. ... Robert Conway, A.M., and others. London, Alexander Hogg, 1784.*

There is a second edition: THE NEW AND COMPLETE ENGLISH TRAVELLER ... *revised ... by William Hugh Dalton, Esq. London, Alexander Hogg, 1794.*

ROBERT SNELL   1785

Size: 36 x 33 inches (915 x 840 mm)   Scale: One inch to one mile

In an ornamental cartouche, top left, is the inscription: *To the Nobility, Gentry, Clergy and Others, this Map of the County* (of Monmouthshire) *is Most Humbly Inscribed by ... Robert Snell.*

A short description of the County to the right of the cartouche.   The arms of Monmouth, top right. Lower part of map: Explanation; Distances of Principal Places; Compass Indicators.

The importance of this map is that it shows in some detail the turnpike roads, relatively new in 1785.

Only two copies of this map are known;   these are in the British Library and the Cambridge University Library.   A facsimile of the Cambridge map is to be found in Monmouthshire Medley, Part III, edited by Reginald Nichols, Starling Press, Risca, Gwent, 1978.

CARINGTON BOWLES   1785

Size: 5.1 x 4.6 inches (129 x 116 mm)   Scale: 9 miles = 1.2 inches

Title, *BOWLES'S REDUCED MAP OF MONMOUTHSHIRE* and Plate number 34 engraved outside the top border.   Remarks, top left.   Compass, top right.   Roads clearly marked.

BOWLES'S POCKET ATLAS OF THE COUNTIES OF SOUTH BRITAIN OR ENGLAND AND WALES, *drawn to one scale ... London, Carington Bowles.* ? 1785.

A map of Middlesex, plate number 33, is printed on the same page.

This map is virtually a reprint of that included in KITCHIN'S POCKET ATLAS, 1769.

ROBERT SAYER   1787

Size: 5.2 x 5.2 inches (132 x 132 mm)   Scale: 10 miles = 0.9 inches

A MAP OF MONMOUTHSHIRE.   Compass, top left.   Scale of miles, bottom right.   Plate no. 27.

The map itself is virtually a reproduction of Jefferys and Kitchin, 1749, following all peculiarities of spelling, e.g. *Crecowel* for Crickhowell.   However, the County information varies somewhat and is differently arranged.   Unlike Jefferys and Kitchin, Sayer describes the Borough of Monmouth and six Market Towns in alphabetical order.   Newport's Fair Days, originally said to be August 15th, November 6th and Corpus Christi Day, are now described as Holy Thursday, Whit Thursday, August 15th and November 6th.

Size: 10.1 x 8.2 inches (257 x 208 mm)   Scale: 6 miles = 1.4 inches

County title, *MONMOUTHSHIRE*, in a panel superimposed on star-shaped compass indicator, top left. *By John Cary, Engraver.* Scale of miles.

Below the border: *London: Published as the Act directs. Sept 1st 1787, by J. Cary, Engraver. Map and Print-Seller, the corner of Arundel Street, Strand.*

John Cary is one of the best and the most productive of cartographers whose work bridges the 18th and 19th centuries. Lacking frills, his maps are very professional productions, usually with outline colour, bringing out essential information with appropriate emphasis by means of bolder lettering on the more important locations. Distances between towns and villages are commonly marked on Cary's maps.

CARY'S NEW AND CORRECT ATLAS: BEING A NEW SET OF COUNTY MAPS FROM ACTUAL SURVEYS. *Exhibiting All the Direct and Principal Cross Roads, Cities, Towns, and most considerable Villages, Parks, Rivers, Navigable Canals, etc ... Printed for John Cary, Engraver, Map and Printseller, the corner of Arundel Street, Strand.* Monmouthshire is plate no. 24.

There were four more editions in 1787, indicating that Cary's NEW AND CORRECT ATLAS was a best-seller. The first three of these are inscribed below the border, simply, *London: John Cary, 1787.* The fifth has again below the border: *Published Sepr 1st 1787 by J. Cary. Engraver and Mapseller, Strand.*

Sixth edition, 1793. Seventh edition, 1793 (when the plate is beginning to show signs of wear and the Monmouthshire map is still dated Sept 1st 1787). Eighth edition, 1795. Ninth edition, later than 1795.

Cary made continual amendments in successive editions. For example, already in 1787, the addition of *Part of Hereford* (*The Futhock*) and *Old Castle* near Llanthony Abbey; additional information along the road from Monmouth to Gloucester; omission of a road from Monmouth erroneously indicated in the first edition as *to the Old Passage* across the Severn and missing it by many miles.

Size: 4.8 x 3.6 inches (122 x 92 mm)   Scale: 6 miles = 0.8 inches

MONMOUTHSHIRE, in panel above map. *By J. Cary*, to the left, and, to the right, *Engraver.* The panel surmounted by a half-compass (indicating West, North and East).

At bottom, distances from London to Newport (147), Caerleon (151), Chepstow (131), Pontypool (150), Usk (144), Monmouth (129), Abergavenny (145). Scale of miles, bottom right.

Below the map: *London. Published Sepr.1.1789 by J. Cary Engraver no. 188 Strand.*

CARY'S TRAVELLER'S COMPANION, *or a delineation of the turnpike roads of England and Wales ... Laid down from the best authorities, on a new set of county maps. London. John Cary, 1790.*

This miniature Cary appeared in a second edition in 1790. There were third, fourth and fifth editions in 1791. According to Fordham, reported by Chubb, there were editions also in 1806, 1810, 1812, 1814, 1817, 1819, 1821, 1822, 1824 and 1828.

There were minor amendments in successive editions. My copy of the edition dated Jan 1. 1821, from *no. 181 Strand*, varies all the distances from London.

The later lithographic transfers, from about the middle of the century, include the earliest railways in the county. In such transfers the map initially may not be changed; the method of printing substitutes lithography, 'writing upon a stone', for engraving, 'cutting into wood or metal'. It follows that there will not be the usual impression mark outside the frame of the map, great pressure upon a plate being no longer required. Revision of the design upon the stone or *lithos* was necessarily frequent in the railway age.

Size: 17.6 x 15.8 inches (448 x 402 mm)   Scale: 6 miles = 3 inches

(69½ Statute Miles to a Degree of Latitude)

The Large Cary. Richard Gough's translation of the 1607 Latin edition of CAMDEN'S BRITANNIA, was issued in 1789. The map of Monmouthshire was engraved by Cary from a drawing by E. Noble. Cary's map is Plate no. 37 in the second of Gough's three volume work.

Later edition, NEW BRITISH ATLAS, *London, John Stockdale, 1805* (also 1809). Substantially the same map as in 1789, but adding later roads.

A MAP OF MONMOUTHSHIRE from the best Authorities. Published by John Stockdale, Piccadilly, 26th March, 1805. Engraved by J. Cary. Reference to Hundreds and compass, top right.

Cary maps of Monmouthshire were used to illustrate David Williams's MONMOUTHSHIRE (1796) (measurements approximately 10 inches height by 8 inches breadth) and, inter alia,   AN ABRIDGEMENT OF MR COXE'S HISTORICAL TOUR IN MONMOUTHSHIRE BY A LADY, 1802 (approximately 8.2 by 10.3 inches).

A NOTE

From Saxton and Speed on through the 17th century the leading engravers and map makers were from the Low Countries. They exalted art and artifice above exactitude. British cartographers like Morden, Kitchin and Emanuel Bowen in the first half of the 18th century came to the fore, seeking greater verisimilitude without sacrificing the picturesque. But in that century, the greatest advance was made by John Cary, whose influence effectively shaped the style of the 19th century Ordnance Survey maps. For example, he first adopted the use of the initial meridian of Greenwich. Cary showed that correctness had a beauty of its own; there is an elegance of art in the precision of science.

Cary's own output was extraordinary. Sir H.G. Fordham estimated that, quite apart from County maps, Cary was responsible for nearly a thousand maps, plans, road-books and other assorted publications. He employed five surveyors who measured with the perambulator, or odometer, a wheel pushed before the surveyor, some 10,000 miles of road a century after John Ogilby.

JOHN HAYWOOD   1787

Size: 13.5 x 16.0 inches (340 x 405 mm)   Scale: 20 miles = 4.2 inches

(69½ British Statute Miles to a degree)

Bottom left: *A MAP OF GLOCESTER* (sic) *AND MONMOUTH, Engraved from an Actual Survey, with Improvements.*

Below the bottom border: *J. Haywood delint. London. Engraved for J. Harrison. no 115 Newgate Street, as the Act directs, Nov 1st, 1787.*

Top left, compass indicator and reference to Hundreds in *both* Counties.

That part of the map which comprises the County of Monmouth measures approximately 6 inches in height by 5 inches in breadth. All the English Counties adjoining Gloucestershire are named, as are the two Welsh Counties next to Monmouthshire.

First edition issued as a loose sheet, or in Rapin's THE HISTORY OF ENGLAND ... *continued by N. Tindal.* 1784—89, published by John Harrison.

Second edition, much revised, MAPS OF THE ENGLISH COUNTIES, *with the subdivisions of hundreds, wapontakes, lathes wards, divisions. etc.* 1791. Reprinted 1792 with slightly varied title.

Third edition, GENERAL AND COUNTY ATLAS, *containing forty-seven maps.* 1815.

Size: 12.6 x 10.2 inches (320 x 259 mm)   Scale: 8 miles = 2.8 inches
                                                                69 British Statute Miles to a Degree

A NEW MAP OF MONMOUTHSHIRE From the Best Authorities. Remarks, top left. Scale of miles, centre. Compass, bottom centre. Below the border: *London. Published as the Act directs, May 30, 1789 by J. Murray No. 32 Fleet Street. J. Lodge sc*(ulpsit).

Similar in design and layout to Joseph Ellis, 1765, though larger. The clarity of the engraving exposes fully the errors slavishly copied from Ellis, e.g. *Llanbilleth, Llanbenock.* *Strangle Castle* enlarges upon the error of Ellis's *Stragle Castle*, Wentwood.

THE POLITICAL MAGAZINE, AND PARLIAMENTARY, NAVAL, MILITARY AND LITERARY JOURNAL ... *London, J. Murray, 1782—1790. Printed for R. Butters, no. 79 Fleet Street.*

Another edition - information below bottom border omitted, c. 1795. A COLLECTION OF MAPS OF THE COUNTIES OF ENGLAND, ORIGINALLY ISSUED IN THE POLITICAL MAGAZINE, 1782—90.

JOHN AIKIN   1790

Size: 4.3 x 3.5 inches (110 x 90 mm)   No scale of miles

Above are the approximate measurements (height followed by breadth) of the map itself on a page otherwise blank, except for the title, *MONMOUTHSHIRE.*

Aikin's is merely an outline map, showing only principal towns and rivers.

ENGLAND DELINEATED; OR, A GEOGRAPHICAL DESCRIPTION OF EVERY COUNTY IN ENGLAND AND WALES ... (*by John Aikin*). *Second edition. London, J*(oseph) *Johnson, 1790.*

The first edition of this book contained no maps.

Third edition, 1795; fourth, 1800; fifth, 1803; sixth, 1809.

BENJAMIN BAKER   1792

Size: 9.0 x 7.1 inches (229 x 180 mm)   Scale: 6 miles = 1.25 inches

MONMOUTHSHIRE. Engraved by B. Baker, Islington. Benjamin Baker became one of the chief assistant engravers of the Ordnance Survey.

Scale of miles below title, top left. No compass indicator.

The map gains in clarity what it loses in detail. The number of place-names is reduced, but adequate.

THE UNIVERSAL MAGAZINE OF KNOWLEDGE AND PLEASURE. *London. 1791-97.* This publication echoes the title of Bowen/Hinton/Kitchin, 1752.

A later imprint is from MAPS OF THE SEVERAL COUNTIES AND SHIRES IN ENGLAND. *London. Darton and Harvey, 1804.*

Laurie and Whittle's NEW AND IMPROVED ATLAS, 1807 and 1816, incorporates revised imprints.

NATHANIEL COLTMAN

Size: 16.5 x 14.5 inches (420 x 370 mm)   Scale: 10 miles = 3.75 inches

Title top right: *MONMOUTHSHIRE by Natl. Coltman*. Compass indicator, top left, above *Smith and Jones sculp., Pentonville*. Explanation, bottom left. Note that Rail Roads here are for horse-drawn traffic. Scale of miles, within lower border, centre.

A very clear map, exhibiting a gallant attempt to spell correctly Welsh place-names. Since the map is included, appropriately folded, in Archdeacon William Coxe's TOUR OF MONMOUTHSHIRE, 1800, it seems not unlikely that the above and other maps under the imprint Smith and Jones were published separately as loose sheets before the first appearance of SMITH'S NEW ENGLISH ATLAS, *London, Printed for C. Smith, mapseller, Strand, 1804.*

Olwen Caradoc Evans records Coltman as a contributor to Laurie and Whittle's WELSH ATLAS, 1805.

C. SMITH and E. JONES

1801

Size: 19.5 x 17.5 inches (495 x 444 mm)   Scale: 1 + 7 miles = 4.3 inches

A NEW MAP OF THE COUNTY OF MONMOUTH Divided into Hundreds. London. Printed for C. Smith no. 172 Strand.

Below the title, top left, a compass indicator and the statement: *Jones and Smith sculp 14 Beaufort Buildings, Strand.* Explanation at bottom left and Scale of miles central, within lower border. Reference to Hundreds, top right.

Smith and Jones (or Jones and Smith, rendered variously, Jones being the engraver) became the unacknowledged basis for many later maps of the County.

SMITH'S NEW ENGLISH ATLAS *being a complete set of County maps ... London, C. Smith, 1804.* The maps are, of course, earlier than the Atlas, and some are so dated.

First edition of map, 1801. Second edition, dated *January 6th 1804. Corrected to 1808.* Six imprints dated 1804: further imprints, 1808, 1818, 1821, 1827, 1830, 1832, 1835, 1839, 1846. Subsequent lithographic transfers include railway lines.

COOK and JOHNSON

Size: 3.8 x 6.25 inches (98 x 159 mm)   Scale: 10 miles = 0.7 inches

An outline map reminiscent of Aiken, 1790, but rather more detailed. Top left, key letters *A* to *O*, less *J*, indicating fourteen places on the map. Top right, compass and symbols for roads, rivers and canals. Scale of miles, bottom left.

Below the border, right: *Cook and Johnson sculpt.* It is possible that the author himself drew the map for the two engravers since Manby has signed several other illustrations in his book.

AN HISTORIC AND PICTURESQUE GUIDE FROM CLIFTON, THROUGH THE COUNTIES OF MONMOUTH, GLAMORGAN, AND BRECKNOCK, *etc. By G.W. Manby, Esq. Bristol, 1802.*

JOHN LUFFMAN

1803

Size: Circular map, 2.3 inches diameter (58 mm)   Scale: 5 miles = 1 inch

In four strips clockwise around an outer concentric circle. The title, *MONMOUTHSHIRE; Monmouth Co. Town 128 miles from London;* Scale of miles; *sends 3 Members to Parlmnt.* A little above the outermost circle, top centre, *plate number 23;* below that circle, *Sold by J. Luffman 28, Little Bell Alley, Coleman Street, London.*

Within the map circle are marked the neighbouring Counties and the Severn River. Only eight locations are named: Newport, Caerleon, Pont y Pool, Usk, Chepstow, Abergavenny, Monmouth and, surprisingly, Llanvetherin. Three roads are shown.

A description of the County is printed below the circular map. The second paragraph begins, *The air of this county is temperate and healthy, and the soil fruitful, though mountainous. Its productions are cattle, sheep, goats, corn and timber...*

A NEW POCKET ATLAS AND GEOGRAPHY OF ENGLAND AND WALES, *illustrated with fifty-five copper plates ... By John Luffman, Geogr. London, J. Luffman, 1803.*

Second edition, also 1803. Reprint of second edition, 1806, published by Lackington, Allen and Co. In 1803 (second edition) and in 1806, the plate number 23 almost rests upon the outermost circle.

R. BUTTERS   c. 1803

Size: 4.9 x 3.4 inches (120 x 86 mm)   Scale: 10 miles = 0.7 inches

Many maps in this series have north to the left, the right or bottom. The title of the County outside the bottom border reads normally, but the map of Monmouthshire, complete with compass indicator, is inverted with the Bristol Channel at the top and north at the foot of the map.

AN ATLAS OF ENGLAND. *Printed and sold by R. Butters, no. 22, Fetter Lane, Fleet Street.* ? 1803. The only recorded copy of this Atlas is in the Cambridge University Library. The title-page has: *Price 6s. plain, and 10s. coloured.*

The map is also in THE PICTURE OF ENGLAND *illustrated with correct colour'd maps of the several counties ... by William Green, A.B. London, J. Hatchard, 1804.*

LAURIE and WHITTLE   1806

Size: 8.9 x 7.0 inches (226 x 178 mm)   Scale: 6 miles = 1.25 inches

MONMOUTHSHIRE, Engraved by B. Baker, Islington. The engraver's name is almost erased by a star-shaped compass indicator which is introduced behind the county title, top left.

Below the bottom border: *Published, October 13th, 1806, by Laurie and Whittle, no. 53 Fleet Street, London.* The firm of Laurie and Whittle still survives in East Anglia, specialising in charts.

The main features added in 1806 to the Baker map of 1792 are: the Rail Road (for horse-drawn traffic, that is) from *Sorwy* (Sirhowy) Furnace to the Ebbw and the Brecon and Monmouthshire Canals from the Western and Eastern Valleys, linking at Malpas. Tredegar House, Wentwood Lodge, St. Pierre, Itton Court, Piercefield and other residences are added.

NEW AND IMPROVED ATLAS, *Laurie and Whittle, 1807 and 1816.*

CHARLES COOKE   c. 1806

Size: 4.8 x 4.2 inches (122 x 107 mm)   Scale: 6 miles = 0.7 inches

Hundreds to the left. Compass, top right. Scale, bottom left. Below the border: *The County Town is denoted by red and the respective Hundreds of the County by different Colours which distinctions are peculiar to the superior Edition.*

Herefordshire and Monmouthshire are bound together in the same volume of Cooke. The map of every county is followed by a topographical or statistical description. There are 132 pages on Monmouthshire in general, apart from itineraries, a list of fairs, a bibliography.

THE MODERN BRITISH TRAVELLER, OR TOURISTS' POCKET DIRECTORY ... *By G.A. Cooke ... London, C. Cooke.* ? 1810.

Also entitled TOPOGRAPHY OF GREAT BRITAIN: OR, BRITISH TRAVELLERS DIRECTORY.

Another edition, 1822.

In 1824, in GRAY'S NEW BOOK OF ROADS. *The tourist and traveller's guide to the roads of England and Wales ... By George Carrington Gray.*

Size: 4 x 7 inches (102 x 178 mm)   Scale: 10 miles = 1.4 inches

MONMOUTHSHIRE in which evey (sic) *Parish and Place is laid down containing upwards of 20 Houses.* Below title: list of numbers of towns, parishes (127), houses (8,948), inhabitants (45,582) and other information, including list of six Hundreds. It does not follow that there were on average more than five people to one house; presumably, meaner dwellings were not included. Scale of miles, bottom left; to its right, compass indicator.

Below the border: *Published Jan 1, 1808, by R. Phillips, Bridge Street, Blackfriars, London.* Outside border, bottom right, signature: *Cooper delt. and sculpt.* Signature erased in second edition, also 1808.

A TOPOGRAPHICAL DICTIONARY OF THE UNITED KINGDOM ... *By Benjamin Pitts Capper, Esq. London, Richard Phillips, 1808.* Hodson notes that the title page offers, *the Mapps coloured and done up separately, price 12 s. half-bound.*

There were other imprints of A TOPOGRAPHICAL DICTIONARY in 1813 (Longman, Hurst, Rees, Orme and Browne); in 1825, 1826, 1829, 1834, 1839 (Whittaker and Co.). The Whittaker imprint reads, below the border: *Published by G. and W.B. Whittaker, 13, Ave Maria Lane, 1824.*

G. COLE and J. ROPER   1807

Size: 9.0 x 6.8 inches (229 x 173 mm)   Scale: 7 miles = 1.6 inches

Title in panel in raised top border. Compass, top left. Hundreds, bottom right. Bottom left, detailed key, including *places where Roman coins have been found.* Scale of miles, bottom centre. Mailcoach-roads and canals are clearly indicated.

Within lower border: *Drawn and Engraved under the direction of E.W. Brayley.* Below lower border: *Engraved by J. Roper from a Drawing by C. Cole ... to accompany* THE BEAUTIES OF ENGLAND AND WALES; *London, Published for the Proprietors by Vernor, Hood and Sharpe, Poultry, June 1, 1807.*

Donald Hodson throws doubt on whether this and similarly described maps actually accompanied THE BEAUTIES OF WALES, published between 1801 and 1815. They were either sold separately or bound in THE BRITISH ATLAS, *Vernor Hood and Sharpe,* 1806, 1810; in ENGLISH TOPOGRAPHY, *Baldwin, Cradock and Joy,* two imprints in 1816; in ENGLISH TOPOGRAPHY ETC ... *By the Rev. J. Nightingale, James Goodwin and Thomas McLean,* 1827; in CURIOSITIES OF GREAT BRITAIN ... *by Thomas Dugdale antiquarian ... Tallis and Co,* 1838, 1842 (two imprints), 1843 (two imprints). There were two lithographic transfers after 1843, up-dating information especially concerning railways.

SAMUEL JOHN NEELE   1811

Size: 13.9 x 11.9 inches (353 x 302 mm)   Scale: 7 miles = 2.8 inches

MAP OF THE COUNTY OF MONMOUTH Divided into Mineral and Agricultural Districts, by Charles Hassall, 1811.

Top right, reference to the Hundreds and compass indicator. Bottom left, reference to the Colours, etc., and Boundary indicators. Scale of miles, bottom centre. Outside the lower border: *Neele sculpt. Strand.*

One of the earliest maps to give specialised technical information. Five divisions are hand-coloured: mineral, indian ink: level, grass green; hill, pale pink; mountain, dark brown; vale, pale blue. The colours have usually faded.

The map sets out clearly means of communication to and from the valleys by road, tram-road and canal. Corresponding very closely to the line of the present Heads of the Valleys Road, a dotted line indicates the North Edge of the mineral Basin, or Farewell Rock. This is Millstone Grit, beneath which no coal is found - hence the name.

SAMUEL JOHN NEELE   1812

Size: 9.7 x 7.5 inches (246 x 191 mm)   Scale: 7 miles = 1.8 inches
                                                                  British Statute Miles

MONMOUTHSHIRE in panel, top left, above scale of miles.   Neele's distinctive compass, top right.
Below bottom border, *Neele sculpt., Strand.   Published by James Cundee, Albion Press London
January 1st, 1812.*   Chubb misquotes 1818 as the date of this map.
     Based on Cary.   One of 45 maps in a neatly engraved atlas.
THE NEW BRITISH TRAVELLER; OR, MODERN PANORAMA OF ENGLAND AND WALES
*... By James Dugdale, LL.D., illustrated by a complete set of correct maps.   London, J. Robins and
Co., 1819.*
     Second edition: ROBINS'S ATLAS OF ENGLAND AND WALES, *accurately engraved by Neele,
from the latest surveys.   1819.*

JAMES WALLIS   c. 1812

Size: 4.4 x 3.4 inches (112 x 86 mm)   Scale: 5 miles = 0.55 inches

MONMOUTHSHIRE in panel above border.   Compass, top left.   Scale of miles, top right.   Key in
panel below map.
     Below panel: *London.   Published by J. Wallis, Engraver, 77 Berwick Street, Soho.*   No plate
number.
WALLIS'S NEW POCKET EDITION OF THE ENGLISH COUNTIES OR TRAVELLERS
COMPANION.   *London, J. Wallis.   ? 1812.*
     Second edition: Plate number, 23, added outside border, top right.
     Third edition: Imprint on map altered to: *London, Published by P. Martin, no. 198 Oxford Street.*
MARTIN'S SPORTSMAN'S ALMANACK, KALENDER, AND TRAVELLERS GUIDE ... *Simpkin
and Marshall, 1818 and 1819.*
     Fourth edition: Imprint removed. LEWIS'S NEW TRAVELLERS GUIDE ... *London, W. Lewis.*
? 1819.
     Fifth edition: Imprint - *London.   Publish'd by W. Lewis, Finch Lane.*   ? 1819, also 1835 and 1836.

EDWARD LANGLEY   1817

Size: 10.1 x 6.7 inches (257 x 170 mm)   Scale: 6 miles = 1.2 inches

     Langley's *NEW MAP OF MONMOUTHSHIRE.*   Compass, top right.   View of Chepstow Castle
engraved, bottom left.   Hundred above.   Scale of Miles, bottom centre.   Key to the right.
     Outside bottom border: *Printed and Published by Langley and Belch, no 173 High Street, Borough,
London, Octr. 1st, 1817.*
LANGLEY'S NEW COUNTY ATLAS OF ENGLAND AND WALES, *embellished with a beautiful
vignette to each map.   London, Langley and Belch.   ? 1818.*
     Second edition.   New imprint: *Printed and Published by J. Phelps, No. 27 Paternoster Row,
London.   1820.*

Size: 9.0 x 7.4 inches (229 x 188 mm)   Scale: 6 miles = 1.4 inches
                                                                                                    British miles

Compass under distinctive Prince of Wales feathers, top left. Scale of miles, top right. Inset in small triangle: *Welch Bicknor, part of Monmouth.* Below bottom border left: *Neele sculpt. Strand.* Title, *MONMOUTHSHIRE,* centre. *Published as the Act directs, May 14th, 1817, by G. Jones.* Based on Cary.
ENCYCLOPAEDIA LONDINENSIS: OR UNIVERSAL DICTIONARY OF ARTS; SCIENCES AND LITERATURE ... *Embellished by a most magnificent set of copper-engravings ... Compiled, digested and arranged, by John Wilkes.* 1810 to 1828; County maps variously dated from 1801 to 1823.

SIDNEY HALL   1820

Size: 4.6 x 2.8 inches (116 x 73 mm)   Scale: 10 miles = 1.5 inches

The title *MONMOUTHSHIRE,* above the border, framed. Compass indicator, top right. Scale of miles, bottom right. Below the bottom border: *Pub. by S. Leigh, 18 Strand. Sidy. Hall sculpt.*
LEIGH'S NEW POCKET ATLAS OF ENGLAND AND WALES, *consisting of fifty-five maps of the counties ... London, Samuel Leigh, 1820.*
Also entitled: LEIGH'S NEW PICTURE OF ENGLAND AND WALES, 1820; and LEIGH'S NEW POCKET-BOOK OF ENGLAND, WALES AND PART OF SCOTLAND, 1825, 1826, 1831.
New imprint below border: *Pub. by M.A. Leigh 421 Strand,* 1831, 1833, 1834, 1835. Signature of Sidney Hall erased 1837, 1839, 1842, 1843.

SAMUEL JOHN NEELE and SON   ? 1820

Size: 6.2 x 5.0 inches (157 x 127mm)   Scale: 6 miles = 0.9 inches

MONMOUTHSH. (sic), in panel top left above scale of miles. Key (including representation of Mail Coach and Turnpike Roads and of Canals), top right. Distinctive Neele compass, bottom right. Outside the bottom border, right, *Neele and Son sc.* (ulpsit) *352 Strand.*
THE TRAVELLERS POCKET ATLAS *consisting of a complete set of county maps, for England and Wales, on an original and improved plan. London, Pinnock and Maunder. ? 1820.*
Second edition adds below border: *Published by G. and W.B. Whittaker, Ave Maria Lane, 1821.*
Third edition removes the Whittaker imprint. From PINNOCK'S COUNTY HISTORY. ? 1825.

W.H. REID   c. 1820

Size: 4.1 x 2.7 inches (104 x 69 mm)   Scale: 6 miles = 0.5 inches

MONMOUTHSHIRE in panel below top border. Above bottom border, from the left: Scale of miles; Key to Mail Coach Roads; Compass.
THE PANORAMA: OR, TRAVELLER'S INSTRUCTIVE GUIDE. *London, W.H. Reid. ? 1820.*
Second edition adds imprint below border: *Published by Hodgson and Co., 10 Newgate Street.*
From THE PANORAMA OF ENGLAND AND WALES. *London, Hodgson and Co. ? 1825.*

Size: 3.4 x 2.3 inches (86 x 59 mm)   Scale: 6 miles = 0.5 inches

Title, *MONMOUTH*, upper border. Ornamental side borders. Statistical information inset in lower border: *The County contains 540,000 Acres, 127 Parishes, 7 Market Towns, 51,274 Inhabitants. It sends 3 Members to Parliament.* The population figure is from the Census Returns of 1811.

THE POCKET TOURIST AND ENGLISH ATLAS ... *London. Printed for O. Hodgson, Maiden Lane, Wood Street. ? 1820. Sheet 24.*

THOMAS DIX   1821

Size: 17.3 x 14.2 inches (443 x 360 mm)   Scale: 6 miles = 2.8 inches

Top left: *A Distant View of Ragland* (sic) *Castle.* In the foreground of the engraving, cattle and a cottage.

Below the view, a key including a symbol for *Parks and Gentlemen's Seats.* At the top centrally, Market Towns and Market Days. To the right of this a Note on the County of Monmouthshire. Lower left, in a circle, the title: *A NEW MAP OF THE COUNTY OF MONMOUTH divided into Hundreds by Thomas Dix.*

Below the bottom border: *London: William Darton; 58, Holborn Hill, Feb. 10, 1821.* Compass central. The six Hundreds, bottom right.

The Note on the County concludes: (Monmouthshire) *was originally considered as a part of Wales and continued so to be till towards the end of the reign of King Charles II when the Judges began to hold the assizes at Monmouth since which time Monmouthshire has been always reckoned an English County. The people use the Welch language, but the English tongue is coming more into use.*

A COMPLETE ATLAS OF THE ENGLISH COUNTIES ...*Commenced by the late Thomas Dix, of North Walsham; carried on and completed by William Darton. London; William Darton, 58, Holborn Hill, 1822.*

Another edition, about 1835, by William Darton and Son. The map of Monmouthshire dated *Feb. 10th, 1830.*

There were lithographic transfers in about 1860 and 1877, adding railways etc.

ROBERT MILLER / 'REUBEN RAMBLE'   1821

Size: 4.2 x 2.7 inches (107 x 69 mm)   Scale: 6 miles = 0.4 inches

Title, *MONMOUTHSHIRE.* Compass and scale of miles, bottom right. Imprint outside bottom border: *London. Published by R. Miller, 24, Old Fish Street.*

MILLER'S NEW MINIATURE ATLAS *containing a complete set of county maps ... London, R. Miller. ? 1821.*

New imprint: *London: William Darton, 58, Holborn Hill.* DARTON'S NEW MINIATURE ATLAS *containing a set of county maps. London, William Darton. 1822 and 1825.*

Lithographic transfers of the Robert Miller maps, designed for children. REUBEN RAMBLE'S TRAVELS THROUGH THE COUNTIES OF ENGLAND. *With maps and historical vignettes. London. Darton and Clark. ? 1845 and ? 1850.* Views are added around the map: Tintern Abbey; Iron Mills; Chepstow Castle. Below title of the County, a symbol for railways appears.

Size: 9.0 x 7.2 inches (229 x 183 mm)   Scale: 20 miles = 2.8 inches

MONMOUTH SH., with half compass indicator above County title. The map is carried over the right border.
Below the bottom border: *Gardner Sculpt. Printed for C. Smith, no. 172 Strand. 1822.*
SMITH'S NEW ENGLISH ATLAS, *being a reduction of his large folio atlas containing a complete set of county maps ... London, C. Smith,* 1822 and 1825.
Second edition, 1828, omits date 1822 in imprint below border.
Third edition, 1844, updates map and was also sold separately as a folding map.

A.N. PERROT 1823

Size: 4.1 x 3.25 inches (104 x 83 mm)   No scale of miles

An amusing French map of Monmouth, Glocester (sic) and Hereford, in which Monmouthshire plays only a small part. Newport, Chepstow, Usk and Abergavenny are the sole locations marked in the County.
The map was drawn by Thierry and engraved by Migneret. The highly ornamented surround has illustrations from hunting, fishing and shooting.
ANGLETERRE, *par A.N. Perrot, Paris. 1823.*

J. THOMPSON 1823

Size: 3.2 x 2.3 inches (81 x 58 mm)   Scale: 6 miles = 0.4 inches

Compass, top left. Title, centre. Ornamental side borders. Very similar to O. Hodgson.
THE NEW ENGLISH ATLAS, *being a complete set of county maps, neatly coloured ...* Sheet 23. *London, J. Thompson, 1823.*

JAMES PIGOT and SON c. 1826

Size: 14.0 x 8.7 inches (356 x 221 mm)   Scale: 10 miles = 3.0 inches

Top right, view of Chepstow Church. Top centre, key. Top left, six Hundreds numbered. Compass below view of Church. Scale of miles, bottom centre.
Below border: *Published by Pigot and Co., 24 Basing Lane, London and 18 Fountain St., Manchester. Engraved on steel by Pigot and Son. Manchr.*
Some detail in adjoining Counties.
PIGOT AND CO., BRITISH ATLAS, ? 1826. Maps also issued separately.
Later editions change address to *Basing Lane* from 1831 and to *59 Fleet Street* from 1839.
Pigot and Son issued a long series of London and Provincial Directories from 1811, covering the whole of the country by 1823. Many of the Directories were accompanied by maps. Mr Brian Stevens, Monmouth, has re-issued the County Directory for 1835 by photo-lithography, complete with Map of Monmouthshire and with additional illustrations using contemporary engravings.
After 1846, the original Pigot maps, with the introduction particularly of railways, appeared under the new title, I(saac) SLATER'S NEW BRITISH ATLAS. 1846, 1847, 1857.
A miniature Pigot (approximately 165 x 100 mm) appears from about 1835 in PIGOT AND CO'S POCKET ATLAS.

Size: 16.3 x 13.4 inches (414 x 340 mm)   Scale: 8 miles + 1 mile = 3.5 inches

Title, *MONMOUTHSHIRE*, top left. Compass, centre. Hundreds, right. Key, bottom left. Scale of miles, bottom centre.

Below bottom border: *London, Published by Henry Teesdale and Co. 302, Holborn.*

Based on Jones and Smith, 1801, and subsequent editions. Clear, detailed map on a scale permitting some indication of street plans of larger towns.

NEW BRITISH ATLAS, *containing a complete set of county maps ... The whole carefully revised and corrected to the year, 1829. London, Henry Teesdale and Co.*

Later, NEW BRITISH ATLAS ... corrected to 1830, 1831, 1832, 1835.

Also lithographic transfers from about 1848. From about 1852, entitled THE BRITISH GAZETTEER.

SIDNEY HALL   1830

Size: 9.6 x 7.4 inches (243 x 189 mm)   Scale: 6 miles = 1.4 inches

Key and compass, top left. Below title, *Engraved by Sidy. Hall.* Below this, the scale of miles.

Imprint outside the bottom border: *London, Published by Chapman and Hall, no. 168 Strand, Oct. 1830.*

A TOPOGRAPHICAL DICTIONARY OF GREAT BRITAIN AND IRELAND, *compiled from local information, and the most recent and official authorities. By James Gorton ... with fifty-two maps, drawn and engraved by Sidney Hall. London, Chapman and Hall, 1831.* There is also a separate folding map.

The imprint outside the bottom border in the second edition, now A NEW BRITISH ATLAS ..., records the date 1833.

Further editions: 1836; 1842; 1843; 1845; 1846; 1847; 1848; 1850; 1852; 1853; 1854; 1855; 1857. The atlas title becomes A TRAVELLING COUNTY ATLAS from 1842. The appearance of railways from the mid-nineteenth century helps to date the maps.

There were later lithographic transfers in 1859; 1860; 1862; 1864; 1866; 1868; 1869; 1871; 1873; 1874; 1875; 1885.

C. and H. (sic) GREENWOOD   1830
(Christopher and John Greenwood)

Size: 22.0 x 27.8 inches (556 x 703 mm)   Scale: 10 miles = 3.6 inches

Top left: *MAP OF THE COUNTY OF MONMOUTH From an Actual Survey made in the Years 1829 and 1830. Published by the Proprietors, Greenwood and Co, Regent Street, Pall Mall. London. Engraved by Josh. Neele, 352 Strand. Corrected to the Present Period and Published Jan 26, 1831.* Below the title, compass indicator.

Bottom left, a view of Tintern Abbey, drawn by R. Creighton (R. Creighton del.). Top right, Reference to Hundreds. Bottom right, Explanation - list of seventeen symbols representing boundaries, divisions, canals, railways, etc.

It is probable that the private surveyors employed by the Greenwoods collaborated with, or even copied from, the public employees of the Ordnance Survey. The Greenwoods had intended to cover the whole country, but failed to publish six English counties.

ATLAS OF THE COUNTIES OF ENGLAND *from actual surveys made from the years 1817 to 1833, by C. and J. Greenwood. London, 1834.*

Size: 17.8 x 14 inches (453 x 356 mm)   Scale: 10 miles = 4.3 inches

Scale and key, top left. Title and six Hundreds listed, top right. Compass, bottom left.

Below the border: *Drawn under the superintendance (sic) of T.L. Murray, 19 Adam Street, Adelphi. Hoare and Reeves sculpt.*

AN ATLAS OF THE ENGLISH COUNTIES DIVIDED INTO HUNDREDS ETC... *projected on the basis of the trigonometrical survey by order of the Honble. the Board of Ordnance ... London. T.L. Murray, 1830.*

Further dated imprints: May 1st. 1831; May 1st, 1832.

Size: 9.0 x 7.0 inches (229 x 178 mm)   Scale: 8 miles = 1.7 inches

Top right, compass below title, *MONMOUTHSHIRE*. Scale of miles, bottom right.

Top left, Reference to the Unions: *1. Abergavenny; 2. Done (sic) (Part); 3. Monmouth (Part); 4. Pont-y-pool; 5. Newport (Part); 6. Cardiff (Part); 7. Chepstow (Part).* The Poor Law Unions, set up following the Poor Law Amendment Act, 1834, are numbered and marked on editions from 1840 on.

Below the bottom border: *Drawn by R. Creighton; Drawn and Engraved for Lewis' Topographical Dictionary; Engraved by J and C Walker.*

A TOPOGRAPHICAL DICTIONARY OF ENGLAND ... *with historical and statistical descriptions; illustrated by maps of the different counties and island ... By Samuel Lewis. London, S. Lewis and Co.,* 1831 and 1835.

Other editions: 1833; 1837; 1840; 1842; 1844; 1845; 1848; 1849.

Size: 10.1 x 7.8 inches (257 x 198 mm)   Scale: 5 miles = 1.1 inches

This is possibly the last Monmouthshire map where it may be said that the decoration is more important than the construction.

There are pleasing views of Tintern Abbey, Chepstow Castle and Monmouth Town Hall. There are three shields bearing Arms. Architectural columns, with figures, in niches enclose the map. A chained swan and unicorn and a burning brazier cluster around the scroll bottom left bearing the title, *MONMOUTHSHIRE*. The scale of miles and the listed Hundreds appear at the top of the map.

Outside the bottom border in the earliest editions appears the signature of the engraver, *W. Schmollinger*.

MOULE'S ENGLISH COUNTIES ... *London, G. Virtue. Simpkin and Marshall and Jennings and Chaplin, 1831.*

Later editions: 1837, 1838, 1839. From 1842, in A COMPLETE AND UNIVERSAL ENGLISH DICTIONARY, *by the Rev. James Barclay* ... Also 1844, 1848, 1850, 1852.

There are very many modern photo-lithographic reproductions of this map, usually betrayed by the nature of the paper and the lack of an impression absent in modern printing methods.

ROBERT K. DAWSON   1831

Size: 9.9 x 8.0 inches (252 x 203 mm)   Scale: 8 miles = 2.0 inches

An outline parliamentary map of the Hundreds with few place-names.
Title, top left, above Population in 1831: 98,200, and Assessed taxes 1830: £14,914.
Compass arrow indicator and scale of miles bottom left. Key, including symbol for polling-places, bottom right.
Signed bottom right, *Robert K. Dawson, Lieut., R.E.*
Printed from lithographic stone in connection with the Reform Bill. Lithographer's name below scale of miles: *Charles Ingrey, 310 Strand.*

SAMUEL TYMMS   ? 1831

Size: 4.9 x 3.0 inches (123 x 76 mm)   No scale of miles

Title, *MONMOUTHSH.*, top centre. Compass, bottom left. Above the border: *The figures show the distance from Monmouth.* Below the border: *Published by J.B. Nichols and Son, 25 Parliament Str.*
A COMPENDIUM OF THE HISTORY OF THE HOME CIRCUIT ... *by Samuel Tymms. London, J.B. Nichols and Sons.* ? 1831 and (with scale 10 miles = 1.0 inches) 1832.
Also included in CAMDEN'S BRITANNIA EPITOMIZED AND CONTINUED ... *by Samuel Tymms. Henry G. Bohn.* ? 1842.

WILLIAM COBBETT   1832

Size: 6.9 x 4.0 inches (176 x 100 mm)   No scale of miles

A simple outline map of the County, indicating only seven towns. Compass, top right. Title, bottom left.
Below the border: *Drawn and Engraved for COBBETT'S GEOGRAPHICAL DICTIONARY OF ENGLAND AND WALES.*
COBBETT'S DICTIONARY was published in 1832. There was a second edition in 1854.

WILLIAM EBDEN   ? 1833

Size: 17.2 x 13.5 inches (436 x 343 mm)   Scale: 5 miles + = 2.2 inches

MAP OF THE COUNTY OF MONMOUTHSHIRE: Divided into Hundreds Containing the District Divisions and other Local Arrangements effected by the Reform Bill. Scale below title, top right. Top left, key and list of Hundreds. Compass star, bottom left. Centre, County members, 2, and symbol for polling-station.
Outside border: *London. Published by J. Duncan. Paternoster Row.*
A NEW ATLAS OF ENGLAND AND WALES ... *London, James Duncan 1833.*
Also, A COMPLETE COUNTY ATLAS ... 1835, 1837, 1838, ? 1845.

JOSHUA ARCHER   1833

Size: 8.9 x 6.4 inches (226 x 163 mm)   Scale: 5 miles = 1.0 inches

White lettering on black background. Top right, Arms of the County. Bottom left, above scale of miles, County title and *London, Edwards, 12 Ave Maria Lane.* Bottom right, *J. Archer sc. Drummond Str., Euston Sq.*

Engraved on a wood-block. Printed by a relief process.

THE GUIDE BOOK TO KNOWLEDGE. *Edited by W. Pinnock. London, W. Edwards, 1833.*

The same map was later issued in black on white in JOHNSON'S RAILWAY ATLAS, 1847.

GRAY and SON   1833

Size: 9.4 x 7.4 inches (239 x 188 mm)   Scale: 6 miles = 1.4 inches

Hundreds and compass indicator, top left. Title and scale of miles, top right. Below the bottom border: *Pubd. by Archd. Fullarton. Engd. by Gray and Son.*

A NEW AND COMPREHENSIVE GAZETTEER OF ENGLAND AND WALES ... *By James Bell ... Glasgow, A.Fullarton and Co. 1833, 1834, 1836.*

In the first editions of some of the 41 County maps in the Gazetteer, there were engraved views of the County in Plate no. 23, Monmouthshire.

The maps were reissued in THE PARLIAMENTARY GAZETTEER OF ENGLAND AND WALES ... *London, Edinburgh and Glasgow,* 1840, 1842, 1843, 1844, 1845, 1846, 1848, 1849. Railways began to be added latterly.

MARY MARTHA RODWELL   1834

Size: 3.0 x 3.5 inches (76 x 89 mm)   No scale

An outline map with numbers and letters, lower-case and upper-case, indicating locations.

The map, together with a map of Herefordshire, faces page 145 in the first Volume of THE GEOGRAPHY OF THE BRITISH ISLES ...*illustrated with separate blank maps and explanatory texts ... By Mary Martha Rodwell. London. Printed for Longman, Rees, Orme, Brown, Green and Longman, Paternoster Row. 1834.*

Each County text takes the form of a dialogue between a mother, Mrs Rowe, and one or other of her two children, George and Anna. George is interrogated on Monmouthshire and receives from his mother some curious information; for example, *Usk* (was) *called anciently Bumbegie. Bumbegie is a* corruption of Brynbuga.

R. CREIGHTON   1835

Size: 9.2 x 7.7 inches (234 x 196 mm)   Scale: 10 miles = 2.5 inches

An outline map, the purpose of which was to give parliamentary information. Hundred boundaries, principal towns and roads are indicated. Copied from Dawson.

Compass, top left. Title, top right. Key, bottom left. Scale of miles, bottom right. Plate LVII, top right outside the border. Outside the bottom border: *Drawn by R. Creighton; Engraved by J. and C. Walker.* Polling stations are marked by Maltese crosses.

A TOPOGRAPHICAL DICTIONARY OF ENGLAND ...*by Samuel Lewis. London, S. Lewis and Co., 1835 and 1837.* Lithographic transfers.

This Creighton map comes from the *SUPPLEMENTARY VOLUME COMPRISING A REPRESENTATIVE HISTORY ...*

Size: 15.1 x 12.7 inches (359 x 323 mm)   Scale: 6 miles + 1 mile = 3.0 inches

(69.1 English miles = 1 degree)

Top left: *MONMOUTHSHIRE, By J. and C. Walker.* County information below title. Compass and inset Welsh Bicknor, top right. Polling places, bottom left.

Below the bottom border: *Published by Longman, Rees, Orme, Brown and Co., Paternoster Row. Feb 1st, 1836.*

BRITISH ATLAS, dedicated first to *Duchess of Kent and the Princess Victoria* and secondly to *Her Majesty Queen Victoria and the Duchess of Kent. London, Longman, Rees and Co. and J. and C. Walker.* Both editions 1837, the year of Queen Victoria's succession.

Further editions: 1839; 1842; 1845 and throughout the 1850's and 1860's. Railway and other additions are drawn by hand to up-date old stocks. Separate folding maps, WALKER'S MONMOUTHSHIRE, dated below the bottom border, on sale up to about 1890.

WALKER'S MONMOUTHSHIRE forms the basis for a series of lithographic Fox-hunting Maps under the series title HOBSON'S FOX-HUNTING ATLAS from about 1850. Only the Monmouthshire Hunt area in the north-east of the County is indicated.

Walker Maps were eventually taken over by Letts.

•   •   •

Later Nineteenth Century Maps of Monmouthshire

COMMUNICATIONS

The earliest published one-inch Ordnance Survey map may be dated 1801, although the surveying was begun in the last decade of the 18th century.

Monmouthshire was surveyed between 1811 and 1820, and again between 1825 and 1831. The first four one-inch to the mile sheets covering Monmouthshire (35, 36, 42 and 43) were published between 1831 and 1833. One type of collector may lament the disappearance of the whimsicalities of earlier less scientifically-based maps; another may welcome the new series that aimed, above, all, at accuracy of measurement and precise if prosaic configuration.

It is not easy to defend all pre-Ordnance Survey County maps, except to say that, while they blundered themselves and copied the blunders of others, they often blundered into a kind of beauty. But clarity and correctness have their own attraction, as collectors of 19th century County maps well know.

Further, the Ordnance Survey series is a splendid primary source of evidence for the historian. There is a graphic representation of the process of historical change as urban and industrial development encroaches upon agricultural and rural Britain.

Whilst the Ordnance Survey maps are all dated, it does not follow that an Ordnance Survey map was published soon after the date on the map. The date imprinted in the bottom margin may have remained unchanged throughout the life of the plate from which it was first printed. Minor adjustments to the plate represented no problem. Obviously, there would have been more frequent imprints in an industrialised County like Monmouthshire, where there was more rapid urban growth after 1800 than in more slowly developing counties.

Of particular interest to the historical geographer is the rapid spread of systems of communication. Roads, such as they were, and canals had already been recorded with some accuracy by private cartographers. They had already included the first tramroads (sometimes misleadingly called by them, rail roads!).

Originally, material for export came down from the hinterland of Monmouthshire by water or by pack-mule over crude ways that were hardly to be called firm, fast roads until after the implementation of the road-making ideas of Macadam from 1815.

The first tram-roads, so-called, were simple parallel rails facilitating haulage over comparatively short distances to rivers or canals by men and beasts. Freight took precedence from the beginning over passengers. The second generation of tram-roads may easily be confused with the first railways, particularly as the cartographical vocabulary was arbitrary.

Dr. Stuart Owen-Jones in RAILWAYS OF WALES makes this distinction: *The use of the word 'railway' is now generally understood to refer to wheels with flanges, running on the edge of a rail. A tram-road, therefore, implies flangeless wheels running on a plate rail which carried a vertical flange.* He illustrates the contrast amusingly by quoting Tennyson, who seemed to think in the full railway age that trains still ran on tram-roads *down the ringing grooves of change.*

Broadly speaking, the appearance of the word "rail-road" on a map of Monmouthshire prior to 1850 indicates the presence of a tram-road.

There was the Merthyr Tram-road, with its steam locomotive, as early as 1804. The Sirhowy Tram-road introduced regular steam-haulage in the 1830's. The Rumney Tram-road of 1836 was the precursor of the Brecon and Merthyr Railway.

The frequent addition of railways proper from the middle of the 19th century called for frequent map revisions, not only in the Ordnance Survey series. Where there is even less satisfactory evidence of the actual, as distinct from the stated, date of maps in the 19th century, some knowledge of the dates of the openings of tram-roads, canals, and certainly railways is desirable. At least one has secure guidance concerning the date before which an undated or imperfectly dated map could not have been printed.

The Monmouthshire Canal from Pontnewynydd was opened for traffic in 1796, entering Newport at the foot of Barrack Hill and terminating in a Canal Basin at the Town Pill, just below the Castle and Bridge. The Canal from Crumlin came in at Crindau in 1798. Work soon began on an extension of the Canal across the Pill, first on to Friars Fields by 1804, and by 1807 on to Tredegar Wharf to be joined by the newly extended Commercial Street and Road, completed in 1810.

The Brecon Canal linked up with the Monmouthshire Canal at Pontymoile, near Pontypool, in 1811. But canals were already obsolescent before the opening of the reign of Queen Victoria in 1837. No more were built as the Great Railway Age dawned.

The South Wales Railway, bringing freight and passengers overland from England through Chepstow and Newport and on to Cardiff and Swansea, was opened in 1850. There were intermediate Monmouthshire stations at Portskewett, Magor, Llanwern and Marshfield. The Severn Tunnel was not to open until 1886.

It was soon obvious that railways were more efficient than any tram-roads, especially when the ten mile an hour speed-limit was lifted in 1852!

In 1852, the Monmouthshire Railway struck north from Newport through Cwmbran to Pontypool. By 1854, one extension had reached up the Eastern Valleys to Blaenavon and another had proceeded via Pontymoile to Abergavenny and Hereford.

By 1857, there was yet another line from Pontymoile near Pontypool through Usk to Monmouth. Caerleon was not linked into the system until 1874 under the auspices of the Pontypool, Caerleon and Newport Railway.

The network of Western Valley railway lines to and from Newport run severally by the Monmouthshire Railway, the Rhymney Railway and the Sirhowy Valley Railway was completed by 1855. The first of these Railways branched at Aberbeeg for Ebbw Vale or for Blaina. The second and third Railways parted company at Bassaleg for Machen and beyond or for stations to Tredegar.

In 1857, the Taff Vale Extension (this Railway had first appeared in Glamorganshire as early as 1840!) cut across the middle of Monmouthshire to Crumlin. There by means of a celebrated viaduct, no longer with us, in 1875 it joined the existing 1855 link from Crumlin to Pontypool.

The Wye Valley Railway opened in 1876. The last rail link of any importance was the Merthyr, Tredegar and Abergavenny Railway across the Heads of the Valleys, completed by 1879, just seven years before the Severn Tunnel in 1886 cut substantially the railway journey from London to Monmouthshire.

Reuben Ramble's Chepstow Castle and Bridge

64

Christopher Saxton, 1577   65

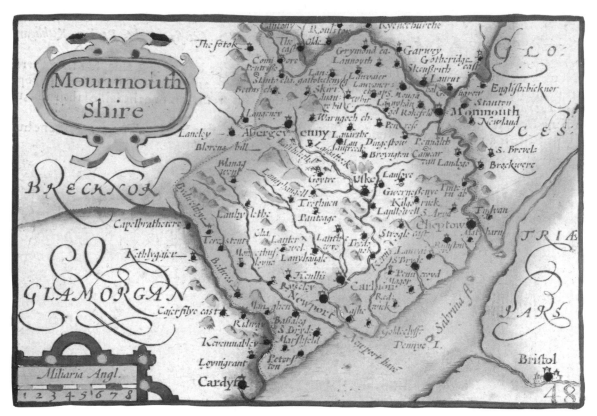

Pieter Van Den Keere, 1627

66   John Bill, 1626

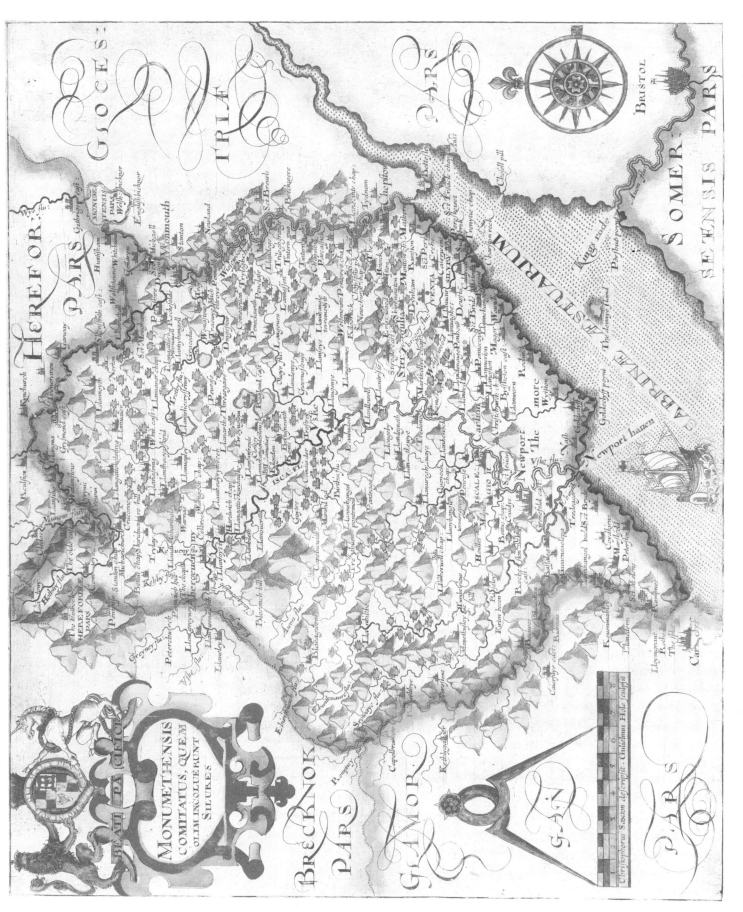

William Camden/William Hole, 1610   67

The Countye of Monmouth with the situation of the Shire towne Described Anno 1610

MONMOUTH

Breknock Shire

A MAPP OF Ȳ COUNTY OF MOUNMOUTH SHIRE WITH HUNDREDS. BY RIC. BLOME BY HIS OWN

PART OF NORTH PART OF HEREFORD SHIRE

BRECK NOCK SHIRE

PART OF GLAMORGAN SHIRE

SEVERN SEA.

SOUTH

A Scale of 4 Miles

Richard Blome, 1673   69

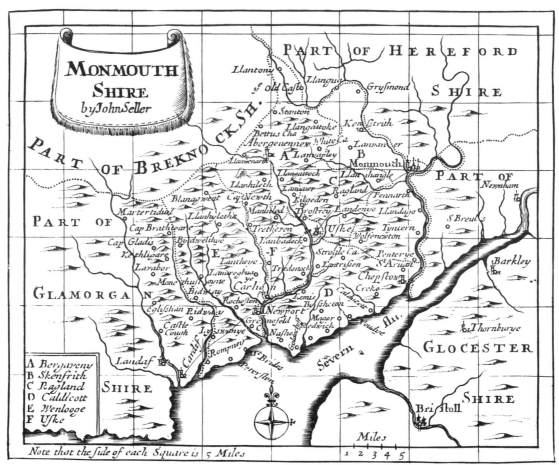

John Seller, c.1694

Emanuel Bowen / John Owen, 1720

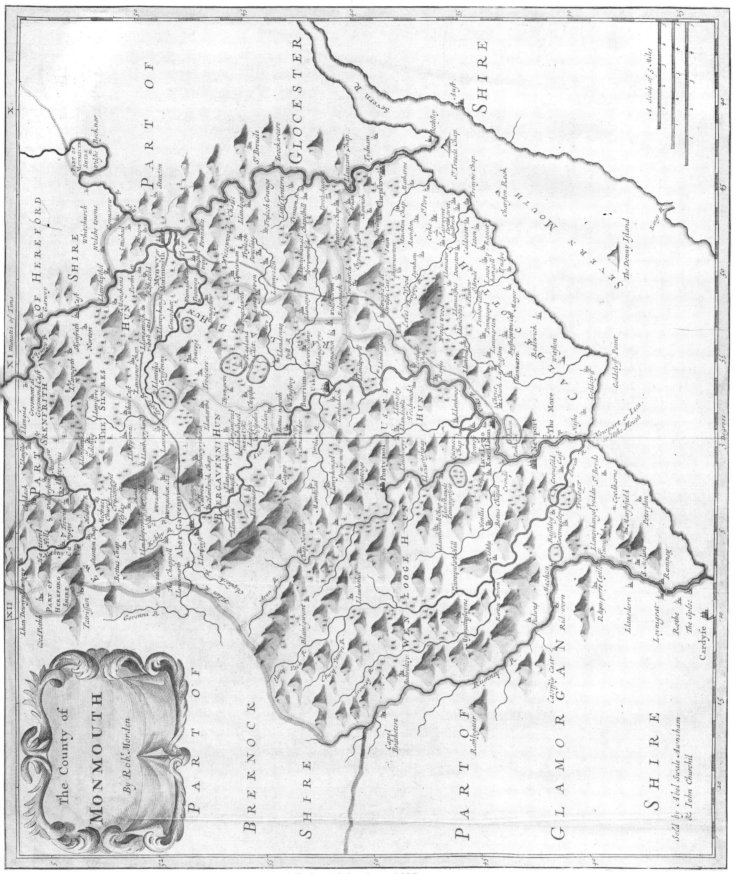

The County of
MONMOUTH
By Rob.t Morden

Sold by Abel Swale Awnsham
& Iohn Churchil

Robert Morden, 1695

71

Monmouthshire sends 3 Members to Parliament, containing one Borough, 6 Market Towns, & 127 Parishes. Monmouth is the County Town, sends one Member, Market Saturday, Fairs August 24. November 11. and Whitsun-Tuesday.

Abergavenny Market Tuesday, Fairs May 3. Sept: 14 and Trinity Tuesday.

Chepstow Market Saturd: Fairs August 1st & Friday before St. Luke.

Kaer Lheion Market Thursd. Fairs May 1st. July 20. Sept: 21. Wednes: before Easter.

Newport Market Saturday Fairs August 15. Novemb. 6. and Corpus Christi day.

Pontypool Market Saturd: Fairs March 11. May 24. June 24. July 29. and September 29.

Uske Markets Monday & Friday. Fairs May 1st. Oct: 18. and Trinity Monday. This County has the River Mynny on the N. Wye on the E. Rhymni W. & the Severn S. The Uske runs thro' the middle of this County, receiving Byrdhin Oilwy & Avon: & Ebwith meets it at the Severn.

PART OF BRECKNOCK SHIRE

PART OF HEREFORD SHIRE

PART OF GLAMORGAN SHIRE

GLOCESTER SHIRE

SEVERN RIVER

English Miles.
5 10

T. Badeslade delin. Publish'd by the Proprietor W.H. Toms Sept. 29. 1742. W.H. Toms Sculpt

Thomas Badeslade / William Henry Toms, 1742

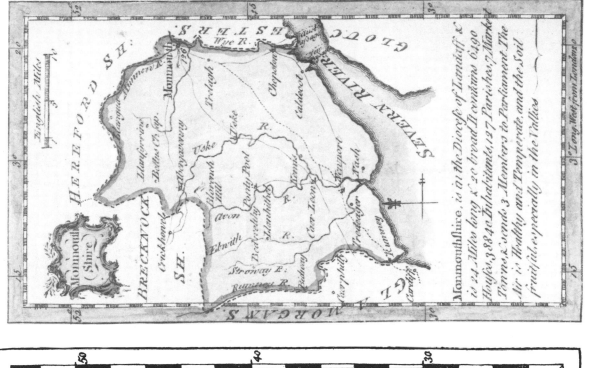

John Gibson, 1759

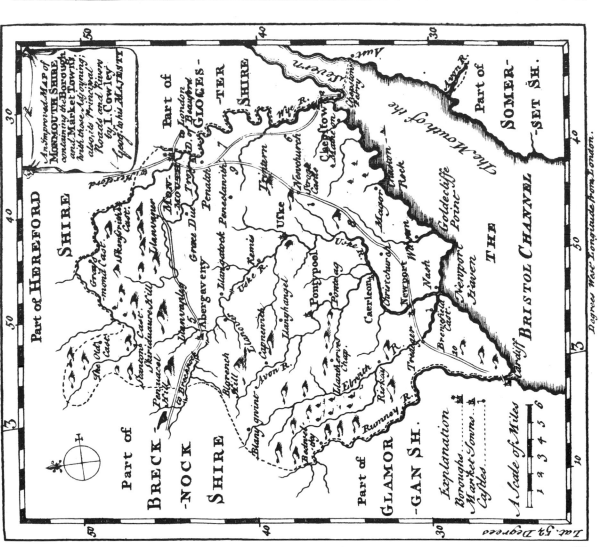

John Cowley, 1744

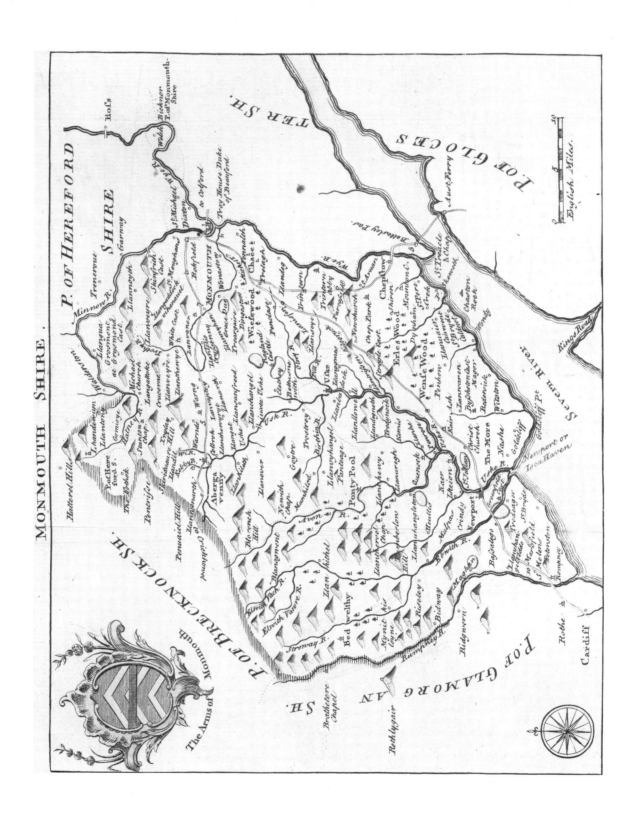

74

Robert Walker, 1746

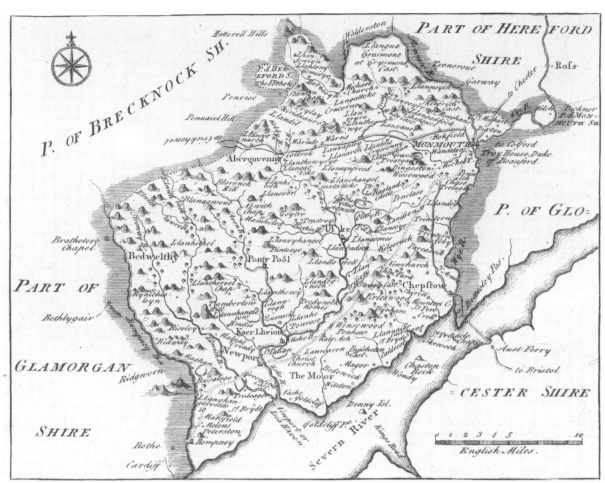

John Rocque, 1746

Thomas Hutchinson / Thomas Osborne, 1748

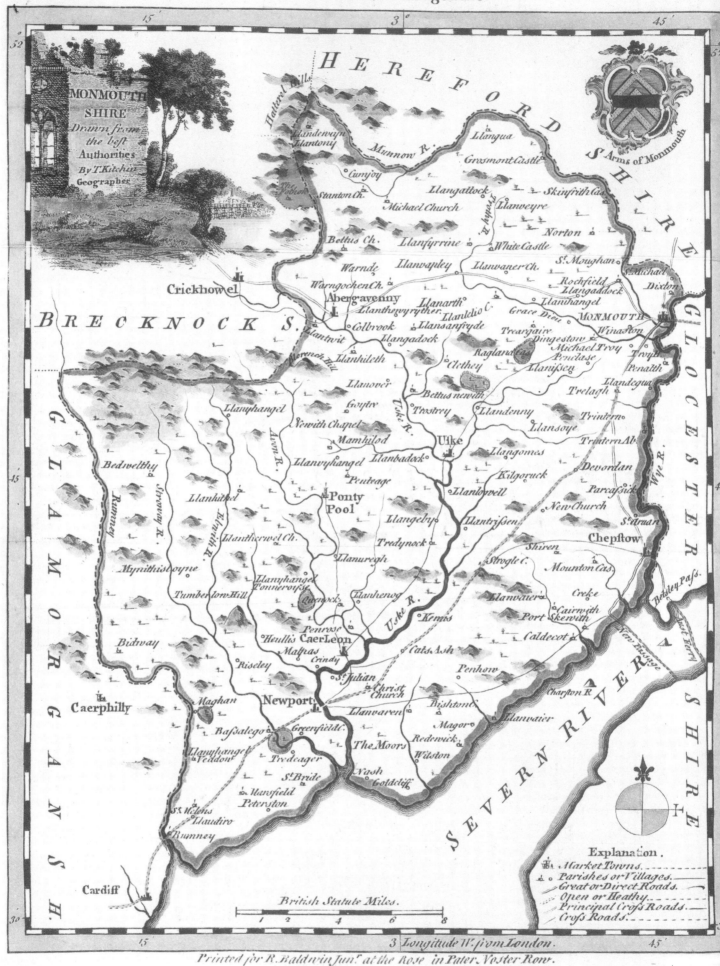

MONMOUTH SHIRE Drawn from the best Authorities By T. Kitchin Geographer

Arms of Monmouth

HEREFORD SHIRE

GLOCESTER SHIRE

BRECKNOCK S.

GLAMORGANSH.

SEVERN RIVER

Hatterel Hills
Llandewyn
Llantony
Munnow R.
Langua
Grosmont Castle
Cunjoy
Llangattock
Skinfrith Cas.
The Poston
Stanton Ch.
Michael Church
Il. capell
Llanveyre
Norton
Bettus Ch.
Llanfyrrine
White Castle
St. Moughan
St. Michael
Warnde
Llanvapley
Llanvaner Ch.
Rochfield
Dixton
Crickhowel
Warngochen Ch.
Abergavenny
Llangaddock
MONMOUTH
Llanthewy ryther
Llanarth
Llanldio C.
Grace Dieu
Llanthangel
Colbrook
Llansanfryde
Treargair
Dingestow
Winaston
Llantwit
Llangadock
Raglan Cas.
Michael Troy
Troy B.
ffrench Hill
Llanhileth
Clethey
Penclase
Llanissen
Penalth
Llanover
Bettus newith
Llandegua
Goytre
Trostrey
Llandenny
Trelagh
Llanvhangel
Newith Chapel
Uske R.
Llansoye
Trintern
Mamhilod
Uske
Llangomes
Trintern Ab.
Avon R.
Llanvyhangel
Llanbadock
Kilgoruck
Devordan
Penteage
Llanloywell
Parcaffuik
Ponty Pool
New Church
Llangeby
Llantriffen
St. Arvan
Llanthewel Ch.
Tredynock
Shiren
Chepstow
Llanuregh
Strogle C.
Mounton Cas.
Bedwelthy
Rumney
Sirwwy R.
Llanhithel
Llanhenog
Llanvaier
Creke
Mynithistoyne
Llanyhangel Tonnerovse
Uske R.
Cairn with Port Skenith
Tumber low Hill
Caernock
Kemis
Caldecot
Bidway
Penrose
Cats Ash
Beisley Pass.
Heullis CaerLeon
New Bridge
Maghan
Malpas
Crindy
Penhow
Aust Ferry
Caerphilly
Riseley
St. Julian
Charston R.
Newport
Christ Church
Bishton
Llanvaier
Baffalego
Greenfieldt
Llanvaren
Magor
Llanvhangel Veddon
The Moors
Redwick
Wilston
Tredeager
St. Bride
Nash Goldcliff
St. Helens
Maysfield Peterston
Llaudiro
Rumney
Cardiff

British Statute Miles.
1 2 4 6 8

Longitude W. from London.

Explanation.
Market Towns
Parishes or Villages
Great or Direct Roads
Open or Heathy
Principal Cross Roads
Cross Roads

Printed for R. Baldwin Jun.r at the Rose in Pater. Voster Row.

Thomas Kitchin / R. Baldwin, 1748

A Map of MONMOUTHSHIRE.

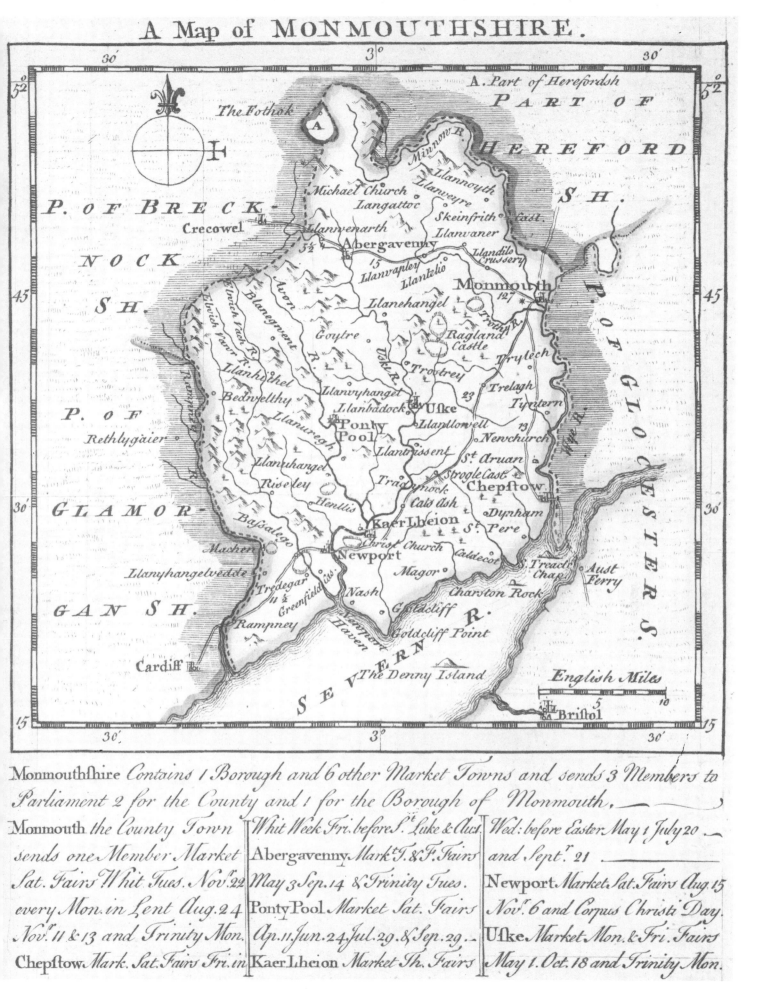

Monmouthſhire *Contains 1 Borough and 6 other Market Towns and ſends 3 Members to Parliament 2 for the County and 1 for the Borough of Monmouth.*

Monmouth *the County Town ſends one Member Market Sat. Fairs Whit Tues. Nov.ʳ 22 every Mon. in Lent Aug. 24 Nov.ˡ 11 & 13 and Trinity Mon.* Chepſtow. *Mark. Sat. Fairs Fri. in*	*Whit Week Fri. before* Sᵗ *Luke & Cus.* Abergavenny *Markᵗ T. & F. Fairs May 3 Sep. 14 & Trinity Tues.* Ponty Pool *Market Sat. Fairs Ap. 11 Jun. 24 Jul. 29 & Sep. 29.* Kaer Lheion *Market Th. Fairs*	*Wed: before Easter May 1 July 20 and* Sept.ʳ 21 Newport *Market Sat. Fairs Aug. 15 Nov.ʳ 6 and Corpus Christi Day* Uſke. *Market Mon. & Fri. Fairs May 1. Oct. 18 and Trinity Mon.*

Thomas Kitchin / Thomas Jefferys, 1749   77

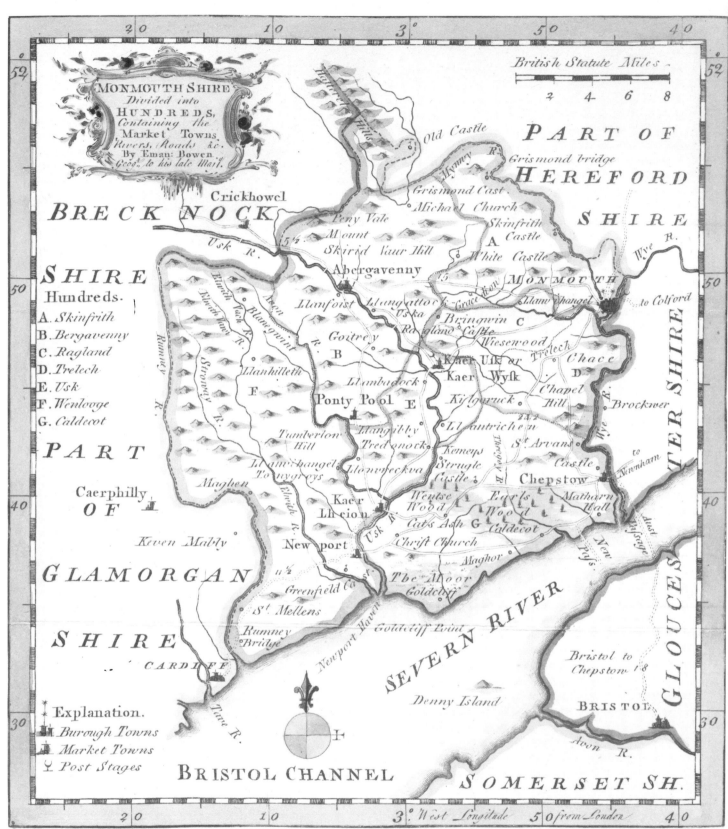

MONMOUTH SHIRE Divided into HUNDREDS, Containing the Market Towns, Rivers, Roads &c. By Eman: Bowen Geogr. to his late Maj.

British Statute Miles

2   4   6   8

PART OF HEREFORD SHIRE

BRECK NOCK

SHIRE

Hundreds.
A. Skinfrith
B. Bergavenny
C. Ragland
D. Trelech
E. Usk
F. Wenlooge
G. Caldecot

PART

OF

GLAMORGAN

SHIRE

Explanation.
Burough Towns
Market Towns
Post Stages

CARDIFF

Crickhowel

Hatterill Hills

Old Castle

Grismond bridge

Mynwy R.

Grismond Cast.

Michael Church

Skinfrith Castle

Peny Vale

Mount

Skirid Vaur Hill

Abergavenny

White Castle

A

MONMOUTH

to Colford

Llanfoist   Llangattock   Grace Dieu

Uska   Llanwihangel

Wye R.

Usk R.

Axen R.

Elwith Vach R.

Blaenewint

Goitrey

B

Bringwin

Ragland Castle

C

Wiesewood

Kaer Uik or Kaer Wysk

Trelech

Chace

D

Llanhilleth

F

Llanbadock

Ponty Pool

Kilguruck

Chapel Hill

Brockuer

Tunterton Hill

Llangibby

Tredonock

Llantrichen

St. Arvans

Castle

to Nawnham

Llamihangel Tonygroys

Llonureckva

Strugle Castle

Kemeys

Wye R.

Maghen

Elwid R.

Kaer Llucion

Wentse Wood

Earls Wood

G Caldecot

Matharn Hall

Chepstow

Caerphilly

Keven Mably

Newport

Cats Ash

Christ Church

Maghor

Dust Passage

New Pass.

Greenfield Ca.

Goldcliff

The Moor

Goldcliff

Bristol to Chepston 18

St. Mellens

Rumney Bridge

Newport Haven

Goldcliff Point

SEVERN RIVER

Denny Island

BRISTOL

Tave R.

Avon R.

BRISTOL CHANNEL

SOMERSET SH.

GLOUCES

Engrav'd for the General Magazine of Arts & Sciences, for W. Owen at Temple Bar 1762.

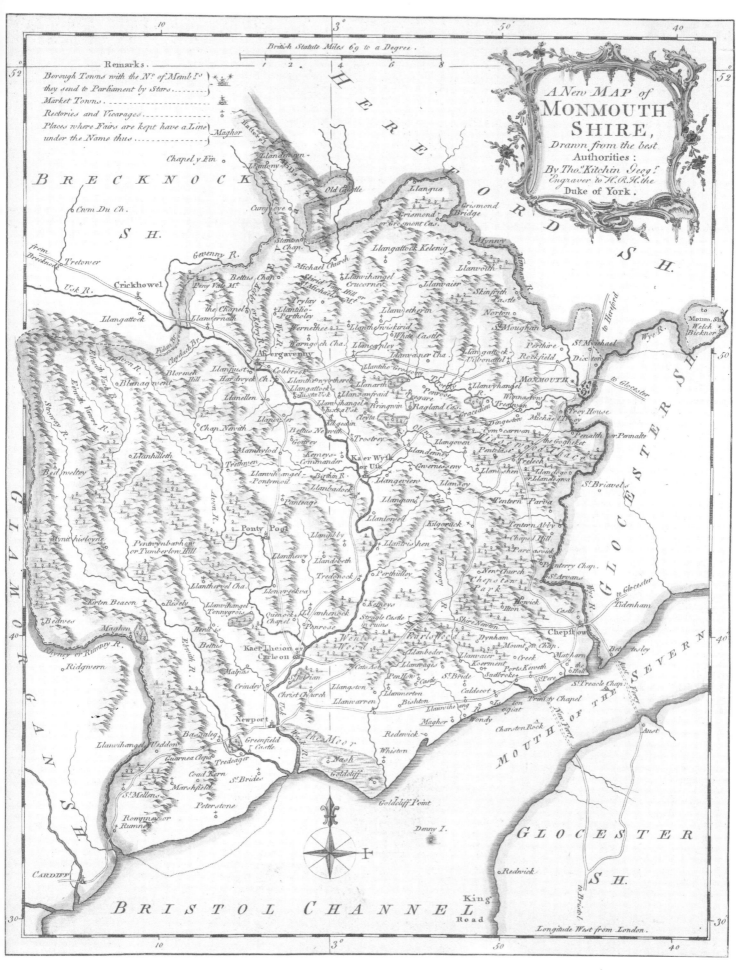

Thomas Kitchin, 1763   79

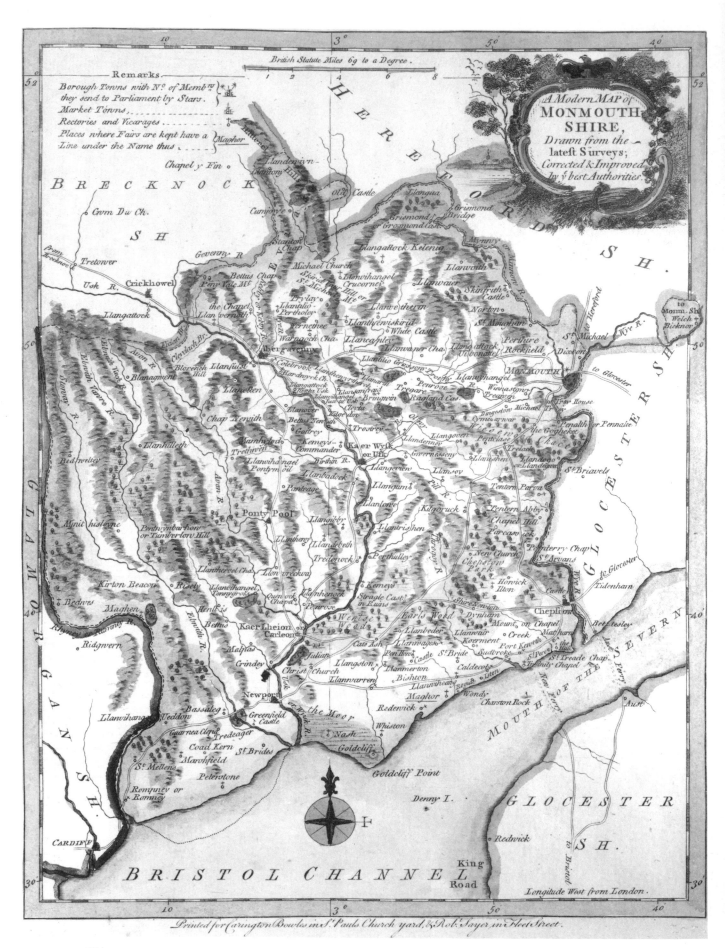

80   **Joseph Ellis / Carington Bowles, 1765**

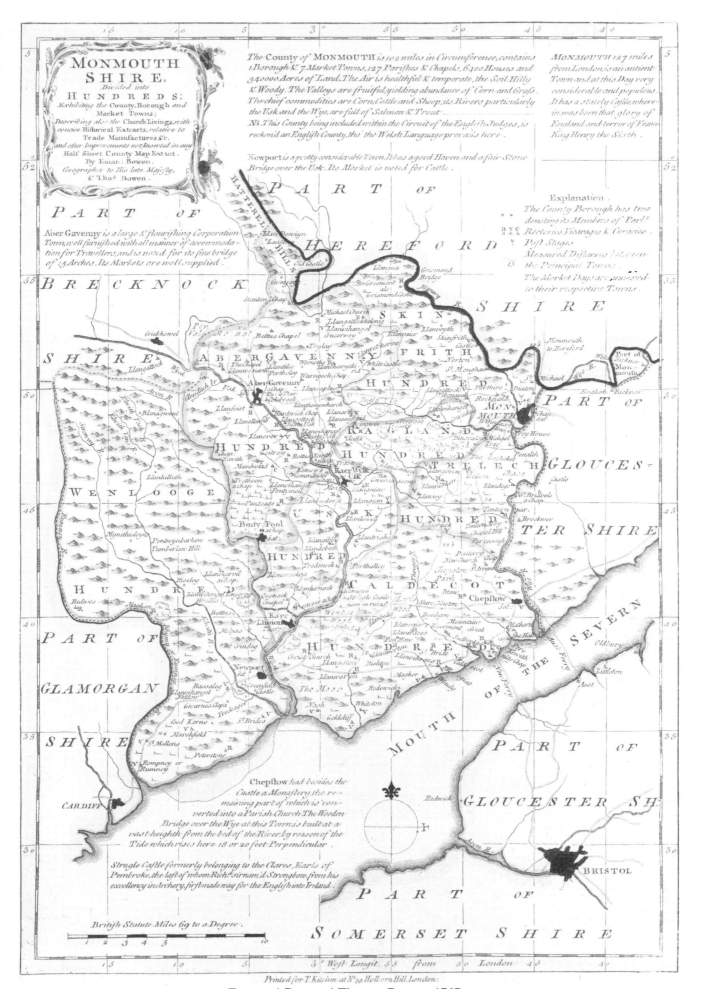

Emanuel Bowen / Thomas Bowen, 1767

81

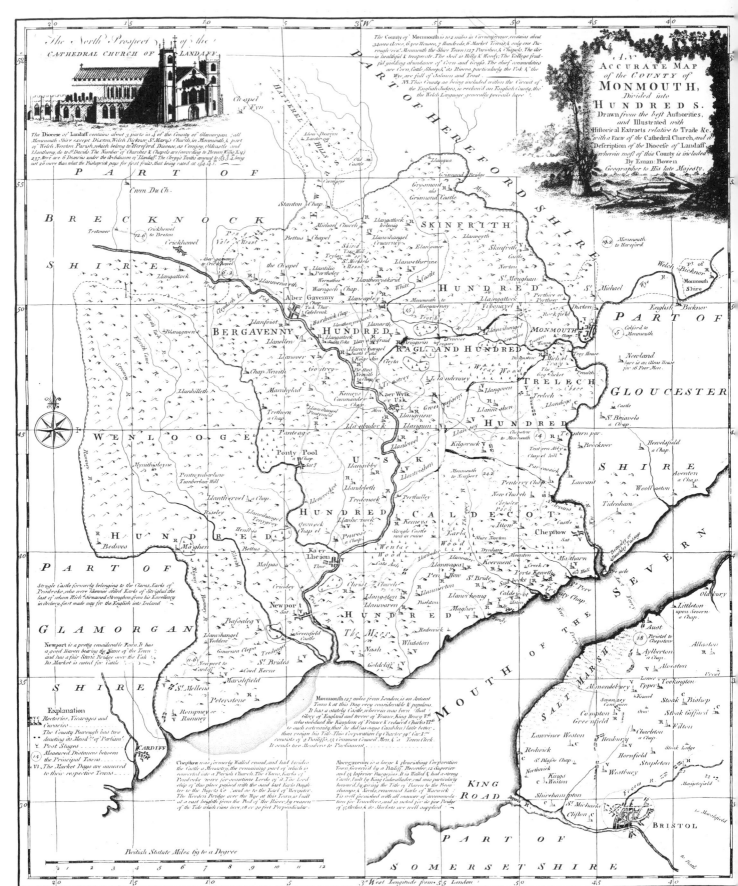

Emanuel Bowen / Sayer et al., 1777

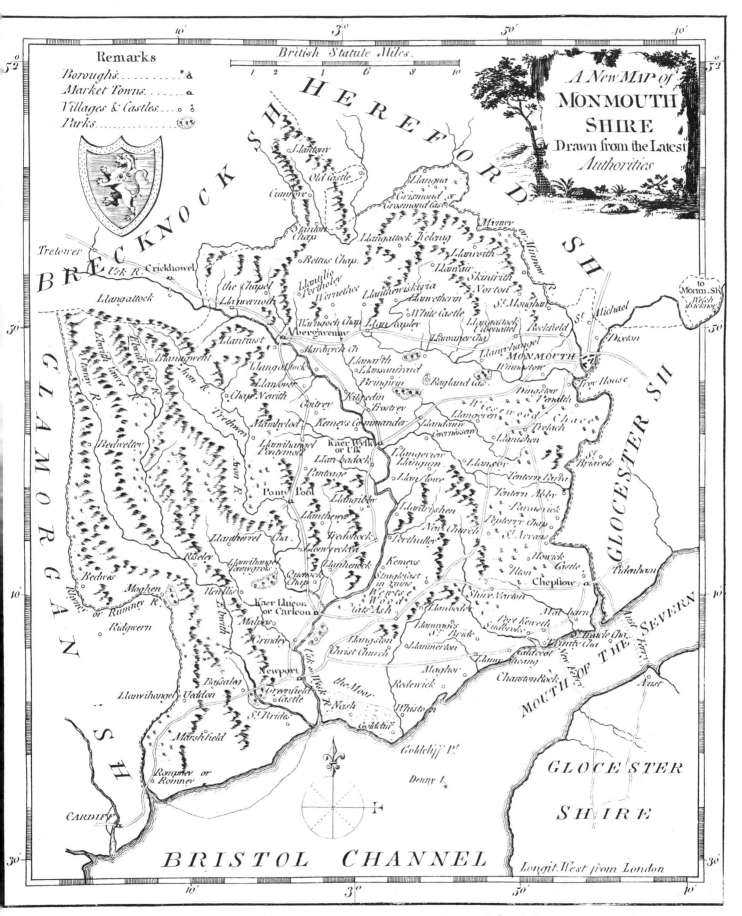

A New Map of MONMOUTH SHIRE Drawn from the Latest Authorities

Published by Alexr. Hogg, at the K

Thomas Conder, 1784

83

MONMOUTHSHIRE.

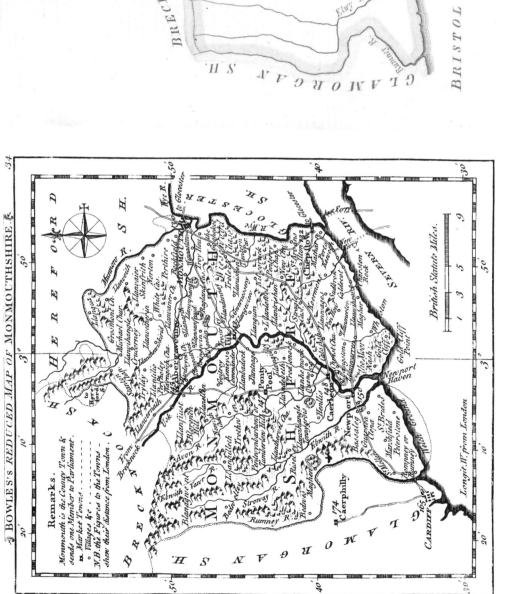

John Aikin, 1790

Carington Bowles, 1785

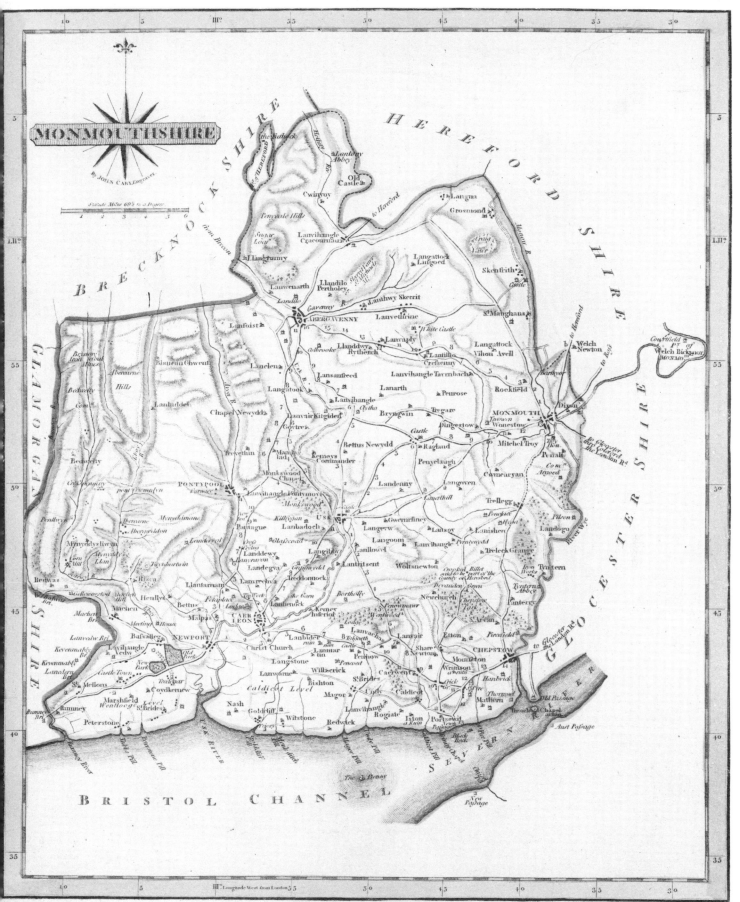

John Cary, 1787

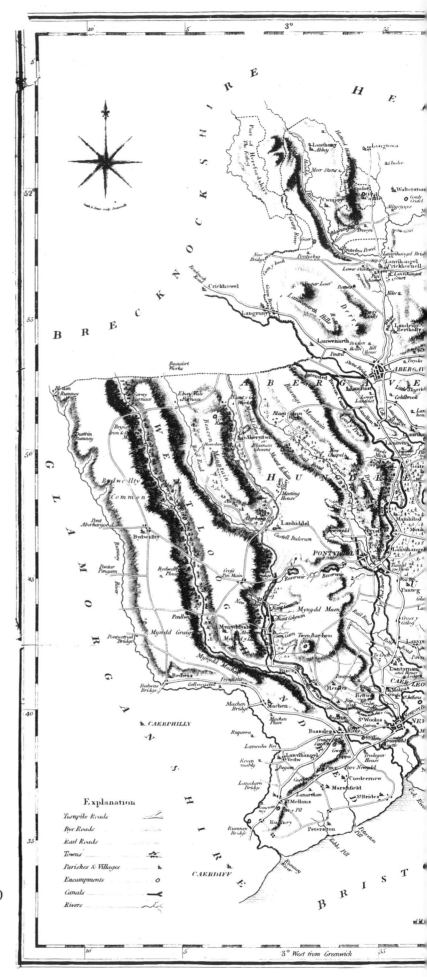

Nathaniel Coltman, ?1790

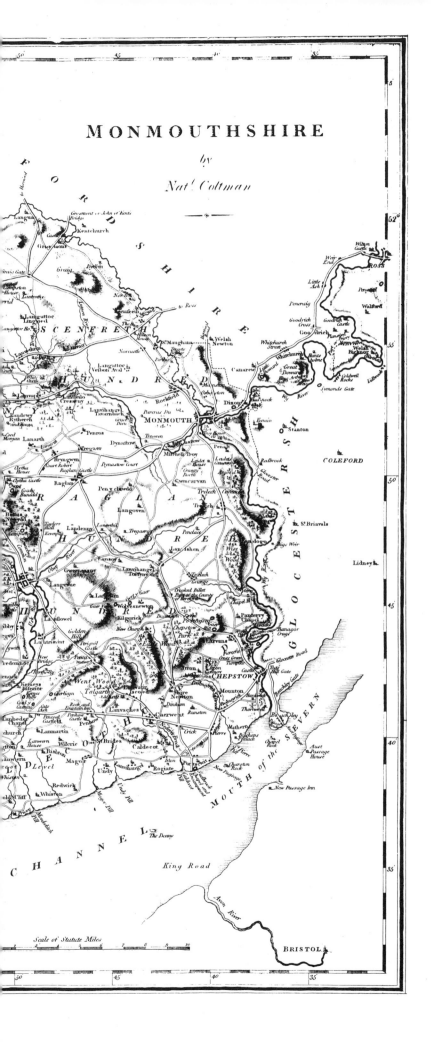

MONMOUTHSHIRE

by

Nat.l Coltman

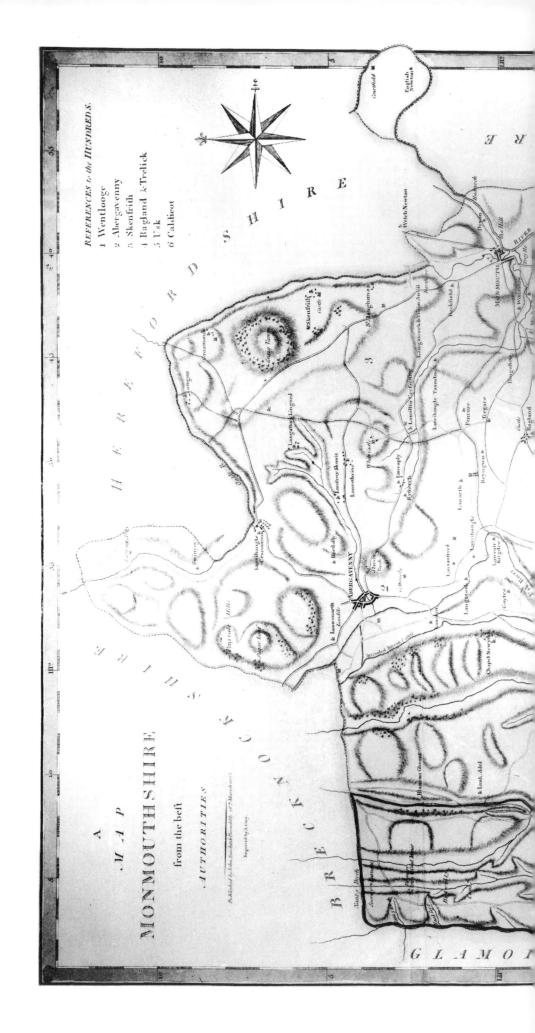

A

M A P

of

MONMOUTHSHIRE,

from the best

AUTHORITIES

Published by John Stockdale Piccadilly 1.st March 1805.

Engraved by J. Cary.

REFERENCES to the HUNDREDS.

1 Wentloogg
2 Abergavenny
3 Skenfrith
4 Ragland & Trelick
5 Usk
6 Caldicot

John Cary / John Stockdale, 1805 (see page 50)

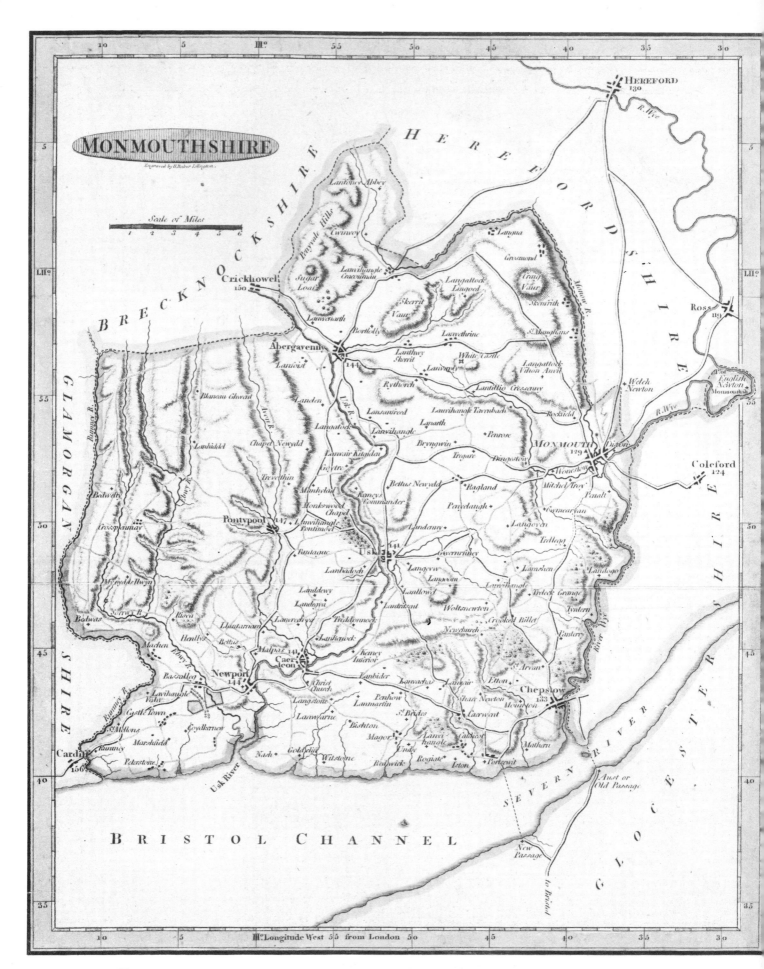

MONMOUTHSHIRE

Engraved by B.Baker Islington.

Scale of Miles
1 2 3 4 5 6

HEREFORD 130

R. Wye

BRECKNOCKSHIRE

HEREFORDSHIRE

Langua
Grosmond
Craig Vaur
Skenfrith

Ross 119

Crickhowel 150

Sugar Loaf
Llanvihangle Crucornin

Skirrid Vaur

Langattock Lingoed

Launworth
Bortilly

Lanvethrine

St Maughans

Welch Newton

Pont English Newton Monmouth

R. Wye

Abergavenny 144

Lantoist

Lanthwy Skerrit

White Castle

Lanvaply

Langattock Vibon Anvil

Rockiield

Blanau Ghwant

Landen

Lansanwreed

Llanvihangle Tavrnbach

Lanarth

Penrose

MONMOUTH 129

Dixton

Lamhiddel

Chapel Newydd

Langatock

Lanvihangle

Bryngwin

Tregare

Dingestow

Wonestow

Coleford 124

Bedwelty

Trevethin

Lanvair Kilgidin

Gogtre

Kemeys Comman.der

Bettus Newydd

Ragland

Mitchel Troy

Paualt

Crosspennnar

Monkswood Chapel

Manhylad

Landeruy

Pandaugh

Camearvan

Pontypool 147

Lanvihangle Pontimoel

Langoven

Trellegg

Mynyddis lhwyn

Rautague

Usk 141

Langeew

Llanvihangle

Landogo

Lanbadoch

Langoon

Tyleck Grange

Bedwas

Piscu

Landewy

Llanllowel

Tyntern

Landegva

Landricant

Woltsnewton

Crooked Billet

Pantery

Llantarnam

Lanvrechva

Treddonnock

Newchurch

Bettws

Lankiock

Malpas 141

Kemey Inferior

Lanvaches

Lanvair

Etton

St Arvan

Machen

Henlly

Caer leon

Chepstow 133

Bassaleg

Newport 144

Christ Church

Lanbider

Shire Newton Moulton

Lavihangle Vahr

Langstone

Penhow

Caerwent

Castle Town

Lanwarne

Lanmartin

St Brides

Coydkernev

Bishton

Lanvihangle

Caldicot

Marshfield

Nash

Magor

Undy

Rogiate

Mathern

Cardiff 156

Rumny

Peterstone

Goldcliff

Witstone

Redwick

Iston

Portscwit

Aust or Old Passage

Usk River

BRISTOL   CHANNEL

SEVERN   RIVER

New Passage
to Bristol

GLOCESTER

GLAMORGAN SHIRE

Rumny R.

Ebwy R.

Benjamin Baker, 1792

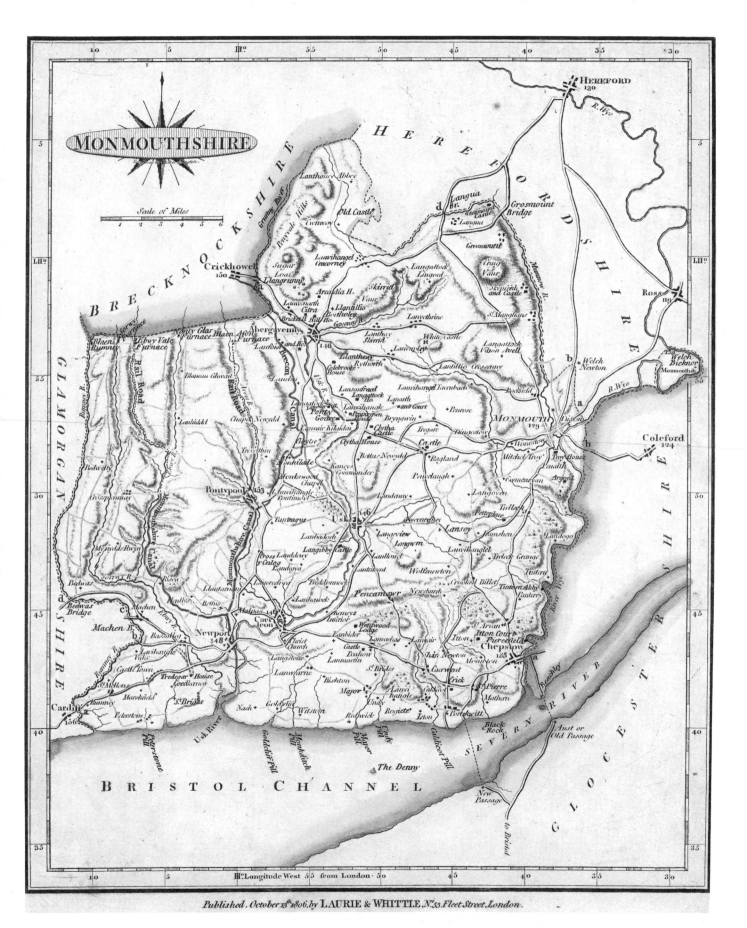

Laurie and Whittle, 1806   91

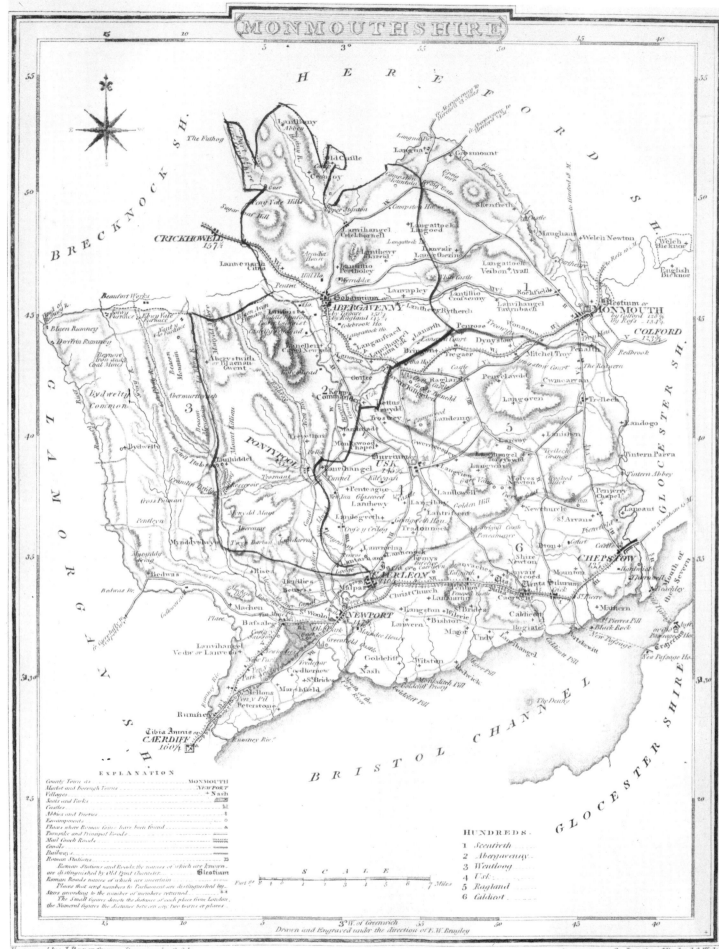

MONMOUTHSHIRE

G. Cole and J. Roper, 1807

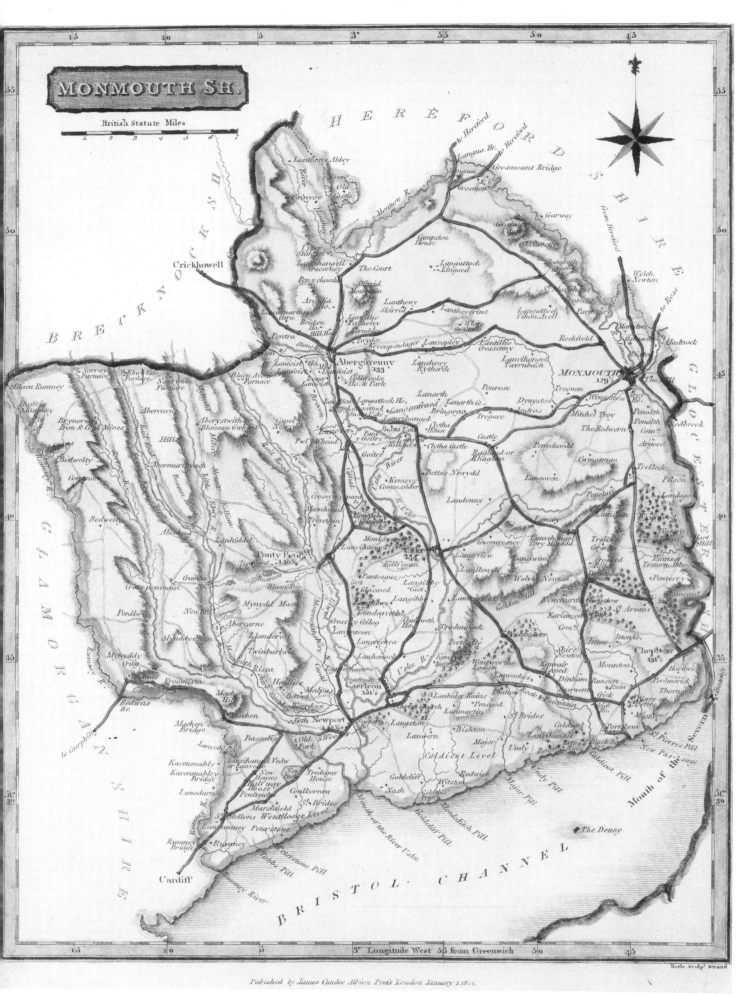

Samuel John Neele / James Cundee, 1812   93

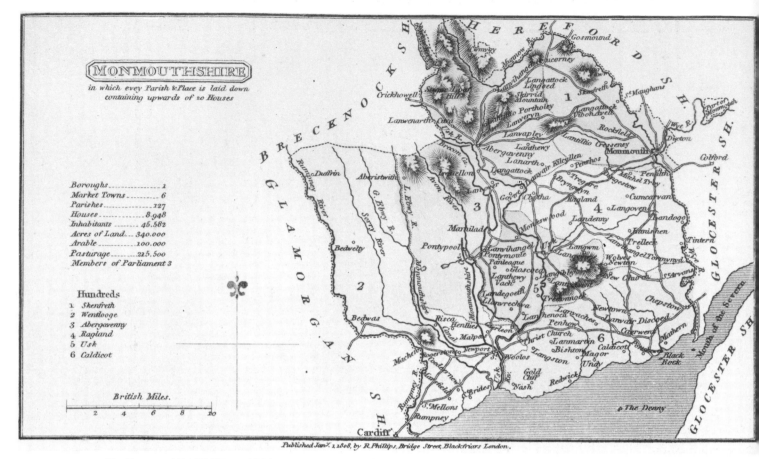

H. Cooper / R. Phillips, 1808

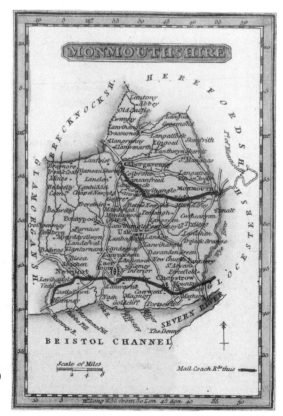

W.H. Reid, c.1820

94

LANGLEY'S new MAP of MONMOUTHSHIRE.

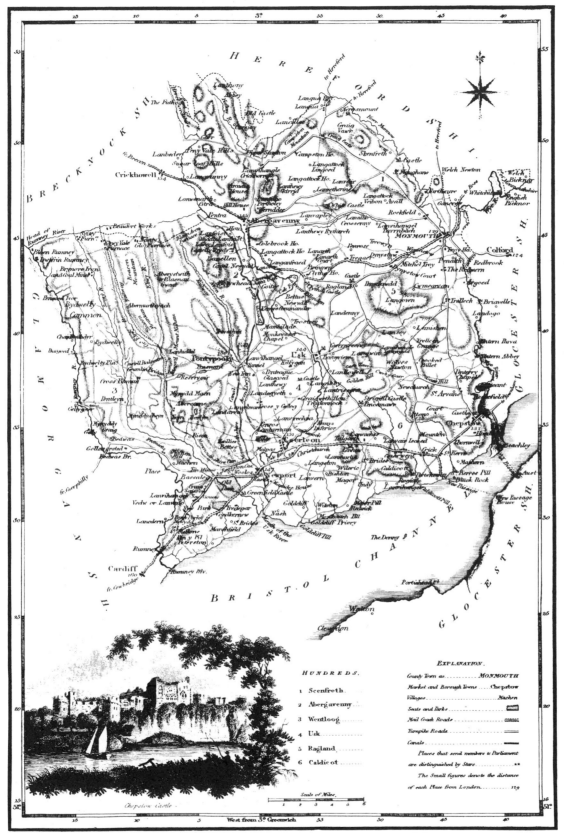

HUNDREDS.

1 Scenfreth.
2 Abergavenny.
3 Wentloog.
4 Usk.
5 Ragland.
6 Caldicot.

EXPLANATION.

County Town as	MONMOUTH
Market and Borough Towns	Chepstow
Villages	Machen
Seats and Parks	
Mail Coach Roads	
Turnpike Roads	
Canals	

Places that send members to Parliament
are distinguished by Stars

The Small figures denote the distance
of each Place from London 129

Scale of Miles.

Chepstow Castle.

Printed and Published by Langley & Belch, No.173, High Street, Borough, London, Oct.r 1.st 1817.

Edward Langley, 1812

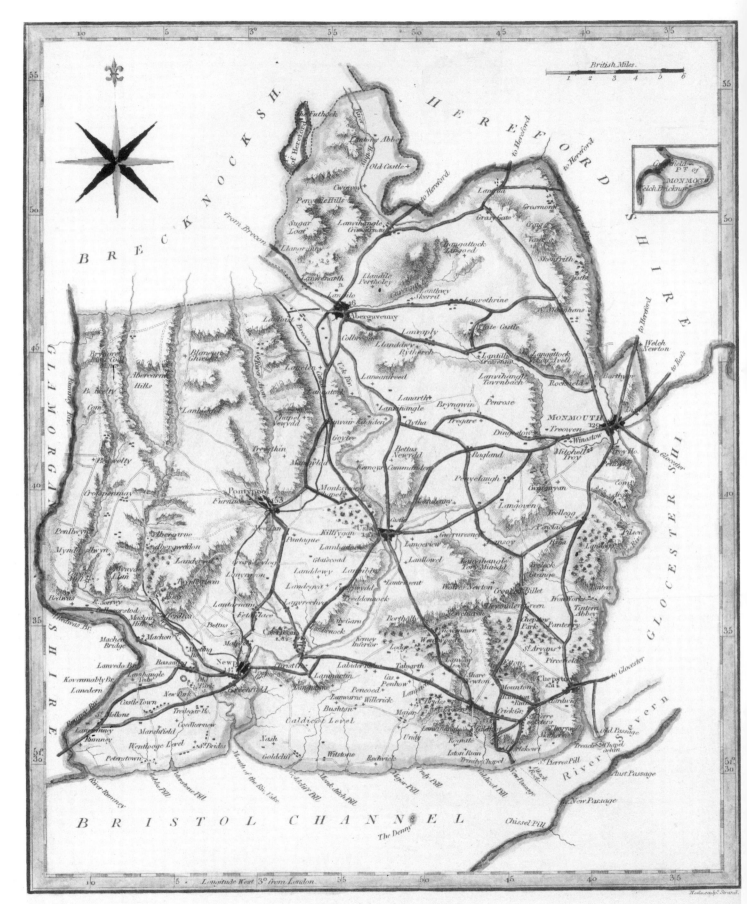

MONMOUTH SHIRE.

Published as the Act directs, May 17th 1817, by G. Jones.

Samuel John Neele / John Wilkes, 1817

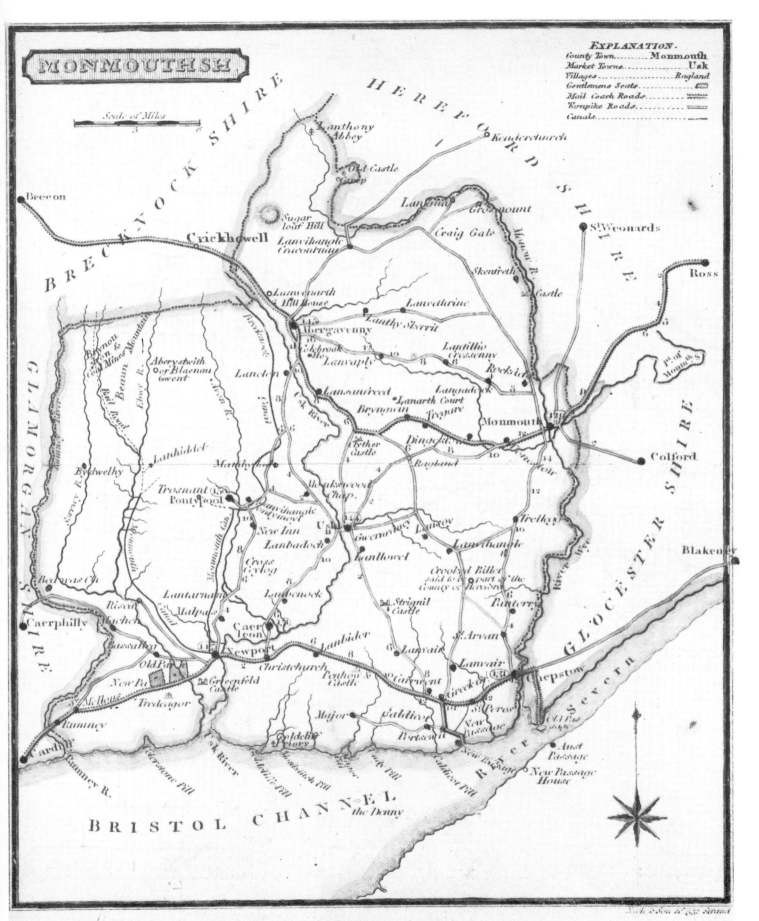

Samuel John Neele and Son / G. and W.B. Whittaker, 1821   97

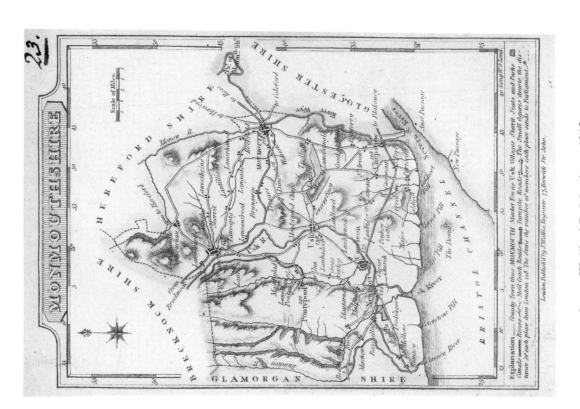

Sidney Hall / M.A. Leigh, 1833

James Wallis / P. Martin, c.1812

98

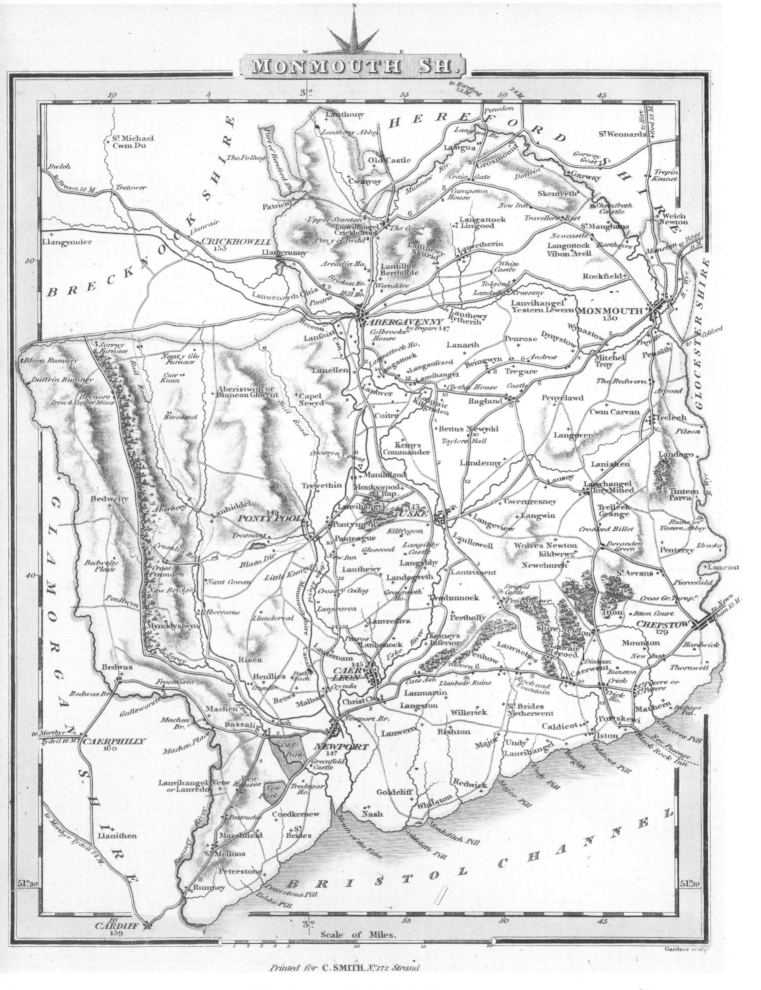

W.R. Gardner / C. Smith, 1828

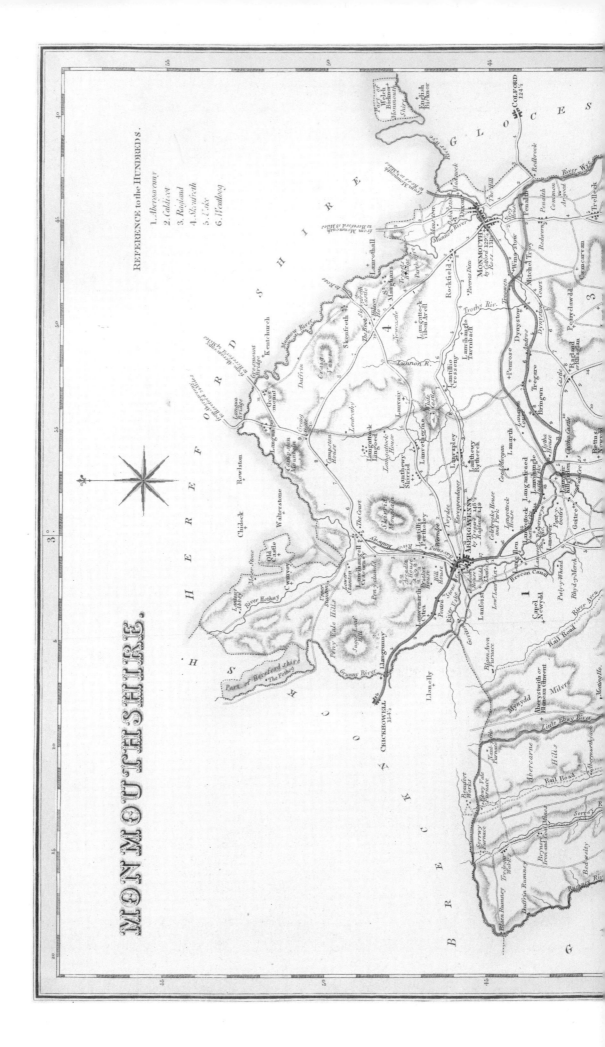

MONMOUTHSHIRE.

REFERENCE to the HUNDREDS.

1. Abergavenny
2. Caldicot
3. Ragland
4. Skenfreth
5. Uske
6. Wenloog

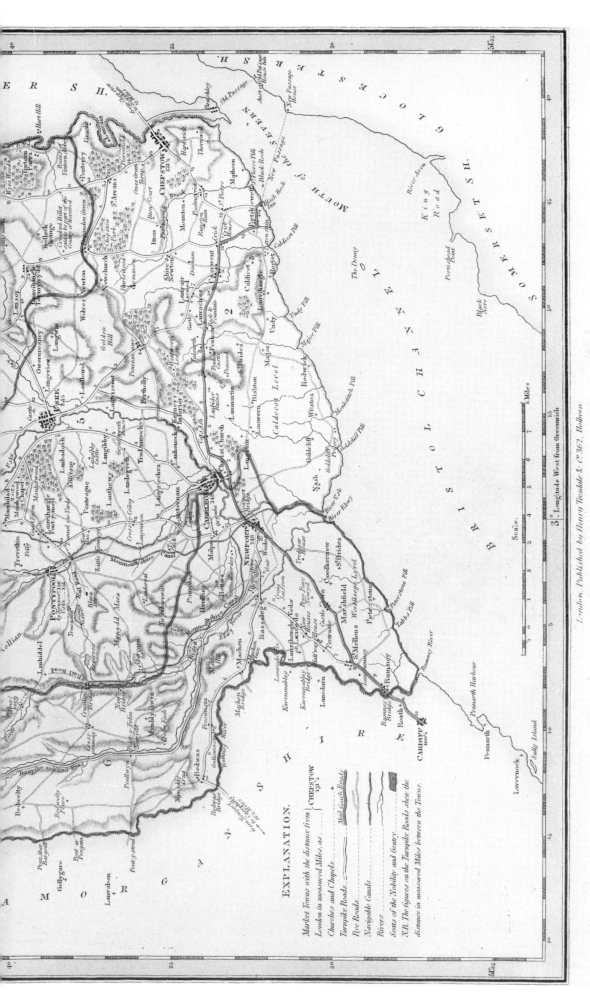

Henry Teesdale and Co., 1829

101

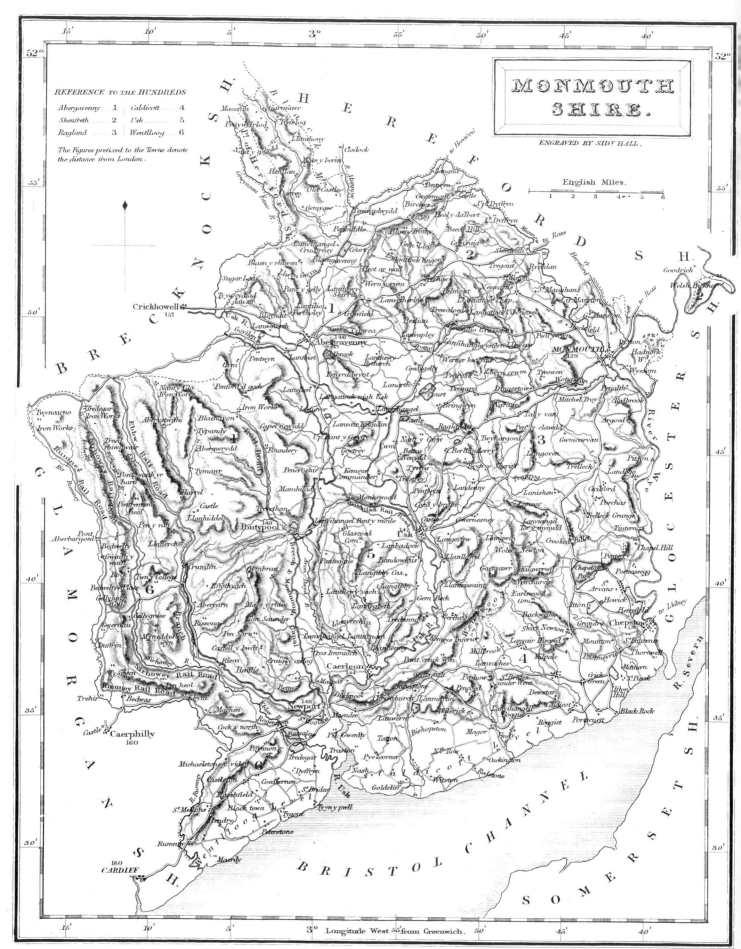

MONMOUTH SHIRE.

ENGRAVED BY SIDY HALL.

REFERENCE TO THE HUNDREDS

Abergavenny	1	Caldicott	4
Skenfreth	2	Usk	5
Ragland	3	Wentlloog	6

The Figures prefixed to the Towns denote
the distance from London.

English Miles.

London, Published by Chapman & Hall, 186 Strand, 1833.

Sidney Hall, 1833

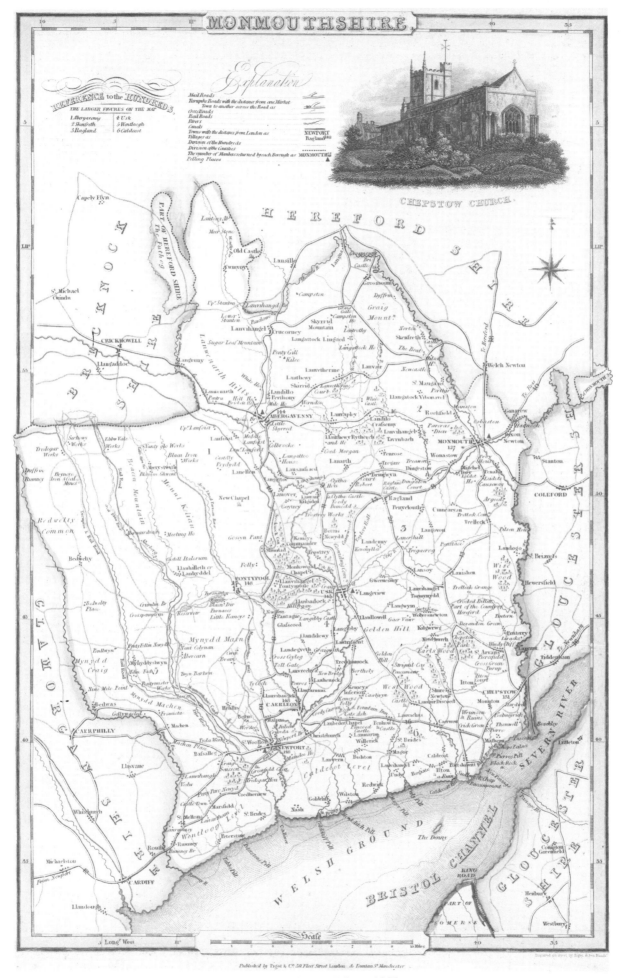

James Pigot and Son, 1839

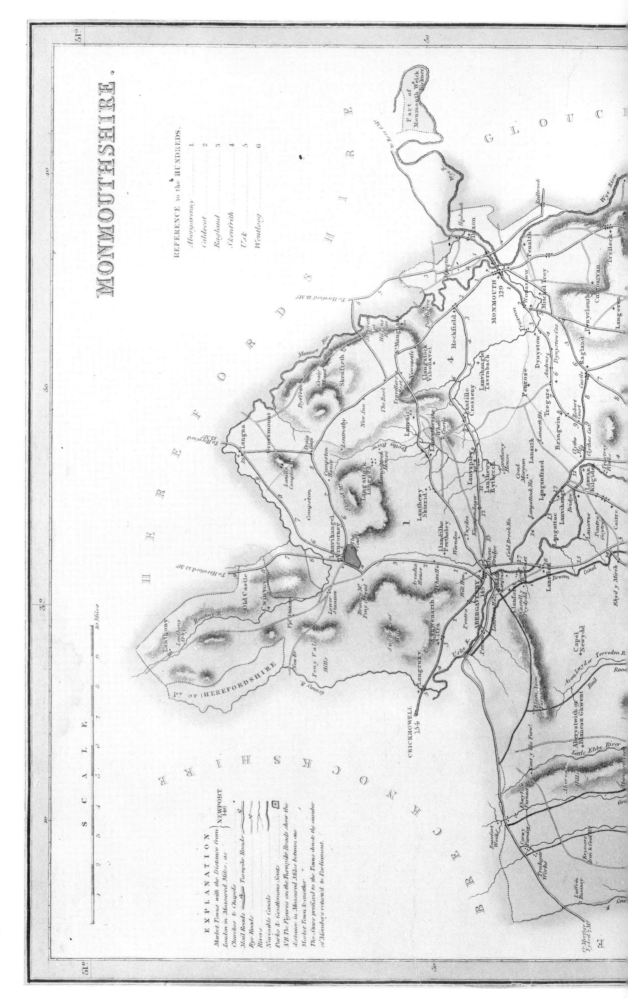

MONMOUTHSHIRE.

REFERENCE to the HUNDREDS.

Abergavenny	1
Caldicot	2
Ragland	3
Skenfrith	4
Usk	5
Wentloog	6

SCALE.

EXPLANATION

Market Towns with the Distance from) NEWPORT 146
London in Measured Miles, as)
Churches & Chapels
Mail Roads
Bye Roads
Turnpike Roads
Rivers
Navigable Canals
Parks & Gentlemens Seats

NB The Figures on the Turnpike Roads shew the
distance in Measured Miles between one
Market Town & another.
The Figures prefixed to the Name denote the number
of Members returned to Parliament.

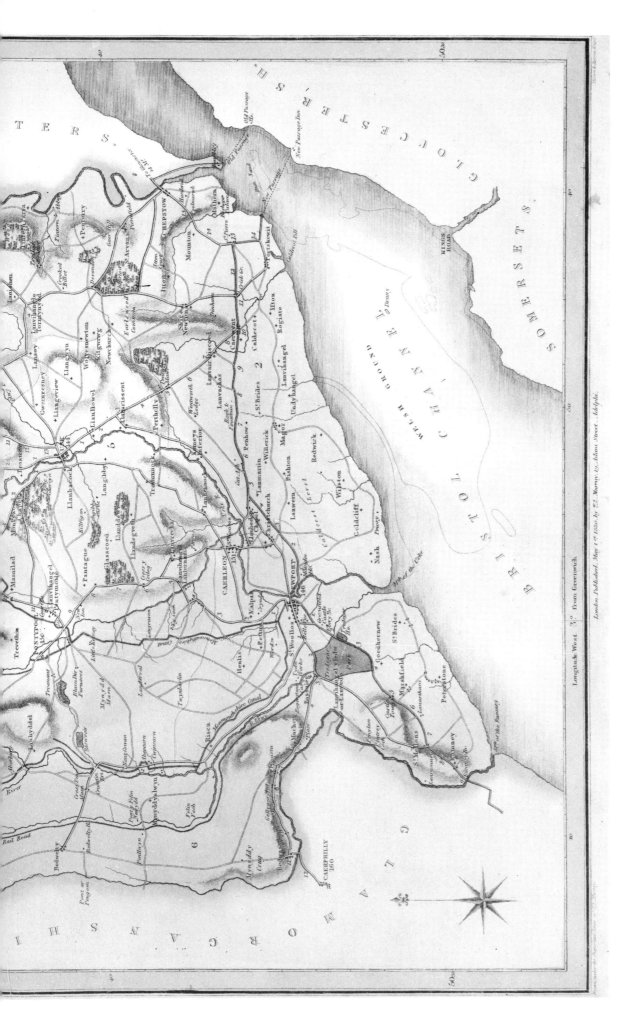

T.L. Murray, 1830

105

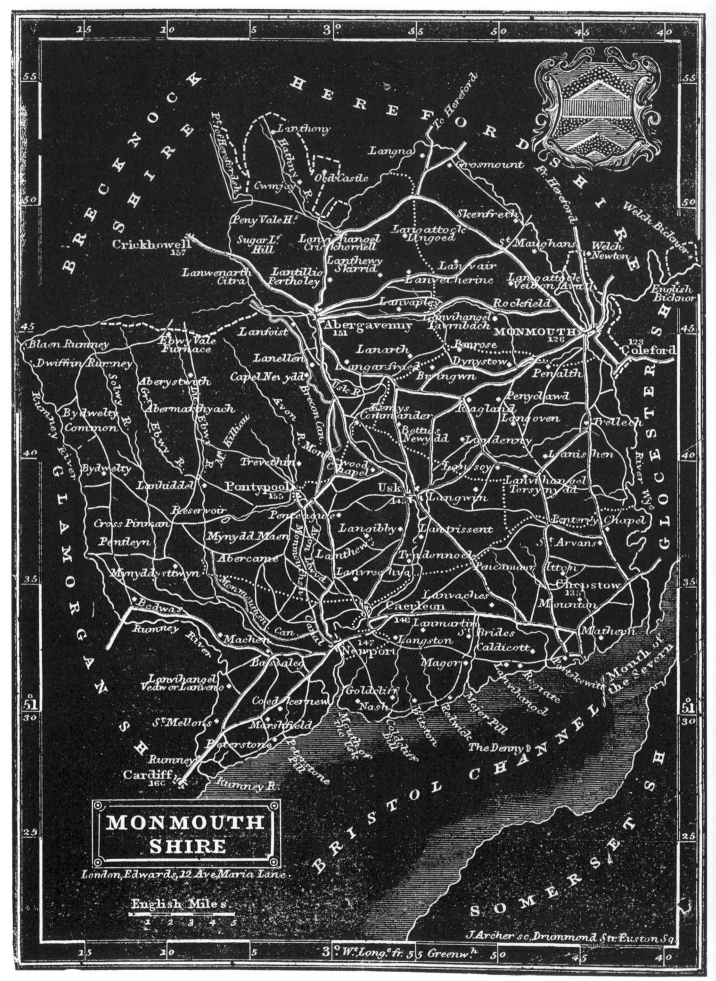

MONMOUTH SHIRE

London, Edwards, 12 Ave Maria Lane.

English Miles.

Joshua Archer, 1833

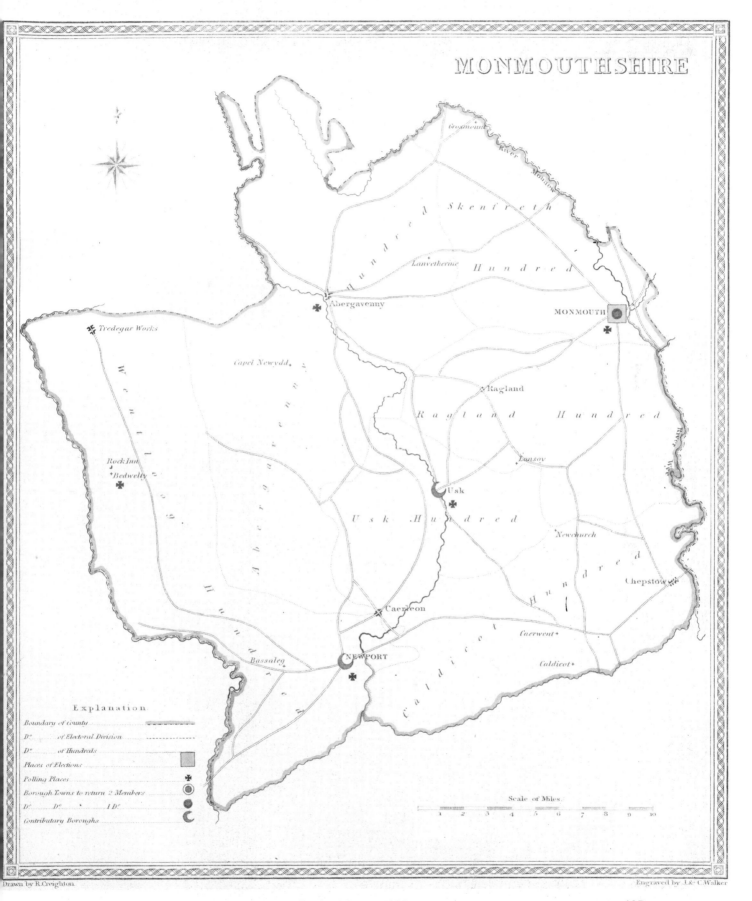

MONMOUTHSHIRE

Groxmouth

River Monnow

Hundred Skenfreth

Lanvetherine   H u n d r e d

Abergavenny

MONMOUTH

Tredegar Works

Capel Newydd

Ragland

R a g l a n d   H u n d r e d

Rock Inn

Lansov

Bedwelty

Usk

U s k   H u n d r e d

Newchurch

H u n d r e d

Chepstow

Caerleon

Caerwent

Bassaleg

NEWPORT

Caldicot

C a l d i c o t   H u n d r e d

Explanation

Boundary of County
Do.   of Electoral Division
Do.   of Hundreds
Places of Elections
Polling Places
Borough Towns to return 2 Members
Do.   Do.   1 Do.
Contributary Boroughs

Scale of Miles.
1 2 3 4 5 6 7 8 9 10

Drawn by R.Creighton.   Engraved by J.& C.Walker

R. Creighton, 1835   107

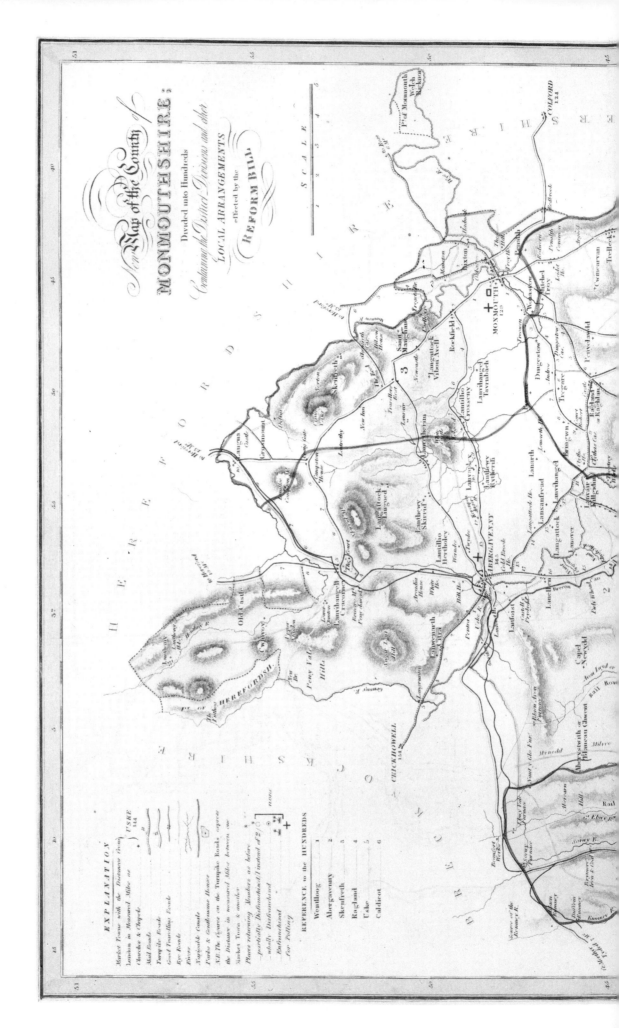

New Map of the County of
MONMOUTHSHIRE;
Divided into Hundreds
Containing the District Divisions and other
LOCAL ARRANGEMENTS
effected by the
REFORM BILL

SCALE

EXPLANATION

Market Towns with the Distances (from
London in Measured Miles are
Churches & Chapels
Mail Roads
Turnpike Roads
Cross Travelling Roads
Bye Roads
Rivers
Noteable Castle
Parks & Gentlemens Houses
N.B. The figures on the Turnpike Roads express
the Distance in measured Miles between one
Market Town & another
Places returning Members as below
partially Disfranchised 1 instead of 2
wholly Disfranchised
Enfranchised
For Polling

REFERENCE to the HUNDREDS

Wentlloog 1
Abergavenny 2
Skenfreth 3
Ragland 4
Uske 5
Caldicot 6

108

William Ebden, 1833

London, Published by J. Duncan, Paternoster Row

County Members 2.   Elections at ☐

3°longitude West fr Greenwich

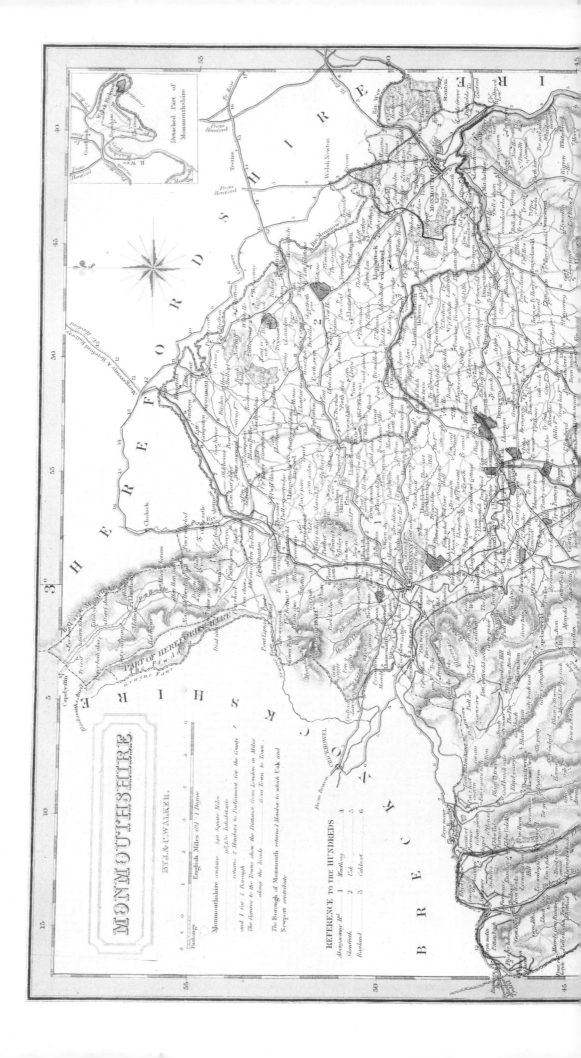

MONMOUTHSHIRE

BY J. & C. WALKER.

REFERENCE TO THE HUNDREDS

Abergavenny H.d	1	Wentloog	4
Skenfreth	2	Usk	5
Raglland	3	Caldecot	6

110

J. and C. Walker, 1836

Index